The Garden of Wisdom

Earth Tales
from the Middle East

For Barbara—

Peace & good wishes ~

Michael D. Caslute

5 February 2018

Green Heart Books
Reading, Vermont, USA

Hardcover ISBN: 978-0-9727518-5-8
Library of Congress Control Number: 2017915195

Publisher's Cataloging-in-Publication data:
Names: Caduto, Michael, J., editor. | Liphshiz, Odelia, illustrator. | Khalilieh, Anton, photographer. | Solowey, Elaine, photographer. | Topel, Elad, photographer.
Title: The Garden of wisdom : earth tales from the Middle East / edited by Michael J. Caduto; illustrated by Odelia Liphshiz; photographs by Dr. Anton Khalilieh, Dr. Elaine Solowey, & Elad Topel.
Description: Includes bibliographical references. | Reading, VT: Green Heart Books, 2017.
Identifiers: ISBN 978-0-9727518-5-8 | LCCN 2017915195
Summary: Original re-tellings of seventeen traditional folk tales gathered from throughout the Middle East, featuring talking animals, adventure, and fantasy.
Subjects: LCSH Tales–Middle East. | Folklore–Middle East. | Ecology–Folklore. | Nature–Folklore. | Earth (Planet)–Folklore. | BISAC JUVENILE FICTION / Fairy Tales & Folklore / Country & Ethnic
Classification: LCC PZ8.1.C134 2017 | DDC 398.2–dc23

P.E.A.C.E.®
Programs for **E**nvironmental **A**wareness & **C**ultural **E**xchange
Website: www.p-e-a-c-e.net • Telephone: 802.649.1815

Quebec-Labrador Foundation: A QLF & Middle East Program for Coexistence

The Stories for Environmental Stewardship collaborative program was made possible by support from:

Quebec-Labrador Foundation
4 South Main Street, Suite #4 • Ipswich, MA 01938 USA
Telephone: 978.356.0038 • Website: www.qlf.org

The Stories for Environmental Stewardship Program received a Brimstone Award for Applied Storytelling from:

National Storytelling Network
c/o Woodneath Library
8900 NE Flintlock Road • Kansas City, MO 64157
Telephone: 800.525.4514 • Website: www.storynet.org

The Garden of Wisdom

Earth Tales from the Middle East

Edited by Michael J. Caduto

Illustrated by Odelia Liphshiz

Photographs by Dr. Anton Khalilieh,
Dr. Elaine Solowey, and Elad Topel

Green Heart Books

Keep me away from the wisdom which does not cry,

the philosophy which does not laugh,

and the greatness which does not bow before children.

— Kahlil Gibran
Lebanese poet and artist

Contents

Stewardship

Wisdom

For Parents & Teachers

Taking Flight

A graceful bird with flowing wings of pure white flies out of a cloud and into the dome of a sapphire sky. Wind rises up and lifts its wings over the snowcapped peak of Mount Hermon, where Syrian bears once roamed.

The egret soars over the blue veins of streams born at the foot of the mountain—waters that flow together to become the River Jordan as it meanders down into the Sea of Galilee, and then to the Dead Sea beyond. From on high, the egret looks far to the west, where waves lap at the shore of a vast sea that reaches to the horizon. It sees green carpets of cedar forest that darken the hills where the land sweeps down into desert swells of rock and sand.

The egret wanders to the south and glides over the steep, rocky cliffs of Gamla on the shore of the Sea of Galilee, where eagles nest and endangered vultures catch rising winds beneath their broad wings. Then it flies further south and west, over the ancient orange groves and natural springs in the Wadi Qana.

Riding a powerful updraft to a great height, the egret turns its eyes toward the west and sees a wide delta where the River Nile empties into the Mediterranean Sea.

Veering off to the east, the egret circles lower and lower, toward a blue-green sparkling eye in the desert—the Oasis of Azraq. With feathers bright in the sun, it spirals down. At last, weary from the long flight, the egret opens its wings into a graceful arch, lowers a pair of yellow feet, and looks down at its own reflection in the water, which seems to rise up to greet it from the surface of the marsh.

After landing, the egret stalks through the shallow water. The surface is a mirror that glows with the warmth of the setting sun. Driven by hunger, it hunts for small fish, frogs, aquatic insects, and other prey. Up near the shore, it sees some strange animals walking on two legs and splashing in the water, and hears them speak a language it cannot understand: words that are not of the kind spoken by those who have wings.

It is a group of children swimming. A moment ago, a young girl, who had noticed a shadow pass between her and the sun, looked up just as the egret glided into the marsh. Now she stares at the egret, and imagines what it would be like to fly through the wide blue sky with the other birds. In her mind's eye, she sets her wings and angles them just so, circling down toward the water. With great white wings held open and long dark legs breaking the surface, she settles gently into the water. Through her eyes as an egret, she imagines that there are no different languages or customs among the birds, as there are in the world of people. There are no countries or borders—just the sun, the wind, and the rain. There are the forests, hills, mountains, and marshes along the shores of the blue oasis. And everything is shared by all living things.

The egret seeks nothing more than a place to rest and feed. It has no thoughts about whether any of the natural areas it has flown over belong to one country or another; nor would it care. From the colorful flocks of migratory birds to the scaly Persian horned viper that slides along the grains of sand—and all things wild—the beautiful land that people call the Middle East is not a giant political puzzle made up of pieces called countries, with their different languages, beliefs, and customs. It is a land of life-giving habitats—a magnificent mosaic of rivers and seas, of forests, mountains, marshes, and deserts, where birds land to rest and feed when flying from their summer breeding grounds in Europe before they make the long, dangerous flight across the Sahara Desert to Central and West Africa. It is the land that everyone shares, that binds all people, plants, and animals together as one.

Unlike the egret, the odd creatures who walk upon two legs have hair instead of feathers, and they are sitting in front of a Bedouin's tent—around an even stranger being with long red tongues that flick at the sky from within a circle of stones. If the egret could understand their strange language, it would hear a storyteller saying, as the gathering of friends and family settles in for the evening, "Who wants to hear a story?"

"I do, I do!" cry the children. "Please tell us a story."

One of the children sees the egret, and silently motions for her friends to look in that direction. Everyone listens as the storyteller begins, but their eyes are following the egret as it moves very slowly through the water, its reflection mixing with those of the reeds bowing in the wind.

It is one of the children's favorite tales—the story of Abu L'Hssein, the Generous. As the action unfolds, the images that appear in the children's imaginations mix with the strange scent of the heat coming off the rocks at day's end, and the soft cooing of a turtle dove that drifts out over the still waters.

(Photo by Dr. Anton Khalilieh)

Animals

Abu L'Hssein, the Generous

-EGYPT-

Abu L'Hssein, the Fox, was trotting along a trail one day when he saw Raven perched in a tree. "Friend, Raven," called Fox, "Would you like to come and visit me? I will give you something good to eat."

"Yes, I would like that," replied Raven.

"Meet me at the rock in front of my den this evening," said Abu L'Hssein as he loped toward home. Once he arrived at his den, Fox began to prepare a meal of porridge for Raven. First, he put some camel's milk in a pot and boiled it slowly over the fire. When the milk was ready, he mixed in some flour and stirred until it thickened.

Raven soon flew in, and landed near Fox.

"Hello," said Fox.

"What are you making?" asked Raven.

"Dinner," replied Abu L'Hssein. Raven, who was very hungry, watched as his friend prepared the meal.

Once the porridge was done, Fox poured it out onto the flat rock on which he was standing. "Here is our meal," he said. "Eat well, my friend."

Raven pecked and pecked at the porridge, but was barely able to eat a tiny morsel. The longer he tried, the more frustrated and hungry he became. Meanwhile, Abu L'Hssein used his tongue to lap up the porridge until his belly was full.

"This foolish Abu L'Hssein," thought Raven. "What kind of friend is he? I cannot eat this way!"

"Abu L'Hssein," said Raven in the friendliest manner he could manage, "you have been most kind and generous by inviting me for this fine meal. Please allow me to repay the favor and prepare a feast for you. I will provide as many sweet dates as you can possibly eat!"

Since sweet dates were Fox's favorite food, he became very excited. "Absolutely!" he cried. "Those dates grow so high in the

date palms that I can only eat the few that fall on the ground and don't get consumed before I happen to find them."

"Excellent," answered Raven. "Meet me at the base of my tree tomorrow at sunset." Raven then flew toward home.

Abu L'Hssein arrived the following evening as the sun was dipping below the distant hills. He saw his friend Raven up in the date palm tree, silhouetted against the orange glow of a beautiful evening sky.

"I am going to knock these dates down for you to eat," Raven called out to Fox. "Get ready to catch them." Raven started picking the sweet dates, but instead of knocking them down where Abu L'Hssein could reach them, he dropped them into the middle of a dense thorn bush.

Fox ran in circles around the thorn bush in search of a way in to gather the dates, but no matter how hard he tried, he could not reach through the thorns to get them. In a short time, his snout was cut up, his lips were red and swollen, and his paws were raw and bleeding from reaching into the thorns.

Raven flew down from the tree. He used his hard beak and scaly claws to pluck one date after another amid the dense thorns. Soon, he had eaten his fill. Raven sat back against the base of the date palm, wrapped his wings around his middle, and groaned with delight.

At that moment, Abu L'Hssein realized what Raven had been doing. Instead of looking upon his friend as inferior, Fox now regarded Raven as an equal. Abu L'Hssein had developed a deep respect for his friend. He realized that although Raven's ways were different from his own, they worked just as well to help him survive.

Red fox *(Vulpes vulpes)*
(Photo by Dr. Anton Khalilieh)

The Hoopoe's Crown

-ISRAEL-

At early dawn, in the setting light of every full moon, King Solomon would mount a majestic white eagle and soar over the mountains. Clearing the high peaks, he would rein in the great bird and veer toward his magnificent palace, which sat high on a bluff overlooking the wilds of Palmyra.

One bright day, King Solomon flew out from the palace on the eagle's back. A relentless sun shone mercilessly on the king's head, causing him to sweat and feel faint.

Just as he was nearly overcome by the searing rays of sunlight, a patch of protective shade was drawn over his head. The king looked up to see a flock of hoopoes using their wings as a shield against the sun's blazing light.

"You have saved my life!" the king cried up toward the hoopoes, who simply tipped their wings to acknowledge the king.

That evening, King Solomon summoned the leader of the hoopoes. "I would like to repay your kindness," said the king. "Tell me what you wish for, and it will be yours."

The hoopoe looked the king over from head to toe, then replied, "My kind have always admired your golden crown. We would have crowns like your own, Majesty."

"So be it," said the king. "But beware, gold is of great value. Hunters and thieves will try to take it from you."

Though they knew of the dangers, the hoopoes could not resist wearing their shimmering crowns of gold. Every time they flew above the surface of calm waters or landed on the edge of a well, the hoopoes gazed down and admired their handsome, glistening crowns.

Their vanity grew. The other birds began to resent the hoopoes, saying, "Those conceited hoopoes think they are superior, just because the king gave them crowns of gold."

Lusting after the hoopoes' golden crowns, hunters began to trap the birds wherever they stopped to admire their reflections.

The hunters used snares. They shot their swift arrows and spears.

The crowns brought such a high price in the marketplace that merchants, peddlers, and even herders abandoned their trades and began to hunt the dazzling birds, melting the gold and molding it into coins and lavish jewelry. In time, the hoopoes were in danger of disappearing forever.

Only then did the leader of the hoopoes return to visit King Solomon to plead for his help. "You were right, My Lord. So many hoopoes have been killed for our golden crowns that we will soon be nothing but a memory. Please forgive our vanity and help us, before the last hoopoe has died!"

"You once saved my life," said the king. "My heart goes out to you and your brethren. It is done. From this day forth, you will not have crowns made of gold. Instead, you will each wear a fine crest of rich golden feathers."

From then on, hoopoes were no longer hunted for their golden crowns, and their numbers grew strong. To this very day, hoopoes wear elegant, fan-shaped crests of feathers. Each feather is tipped with black, because hoopoes still fly high, and sometimes singe their feathers when they get too close to the heat of the sun.

Hoopoe *(Upupa epops)*
(Photo by Dr. Anton Khalilieh)

What Really Happened?

- PALESTINE -

In a big field near a small Palestinian village, there once was an ancient well. The peasants used the well to drink, irrigate the trees, and water the animals. Everyone who lived in the village, old and young, also worked in the field.

One spring day when the lovely almond tree had ripened, one of its small seeds fell and struck Chameleon on the head. Chameleon screamed from the excruciating pain, and quickly ran for help. The pain was so unbearable that she started to cry.

Hearing her cries, Turtle came and asked, "What happened to you? Are you injured?" But Chameleon did not listen or calm down. Chameleon kept crying and walking aimlessly.

Turtle went to find Rabbit, and told him what he had seen. Then he asked Rabbit if he knew what had happened to Chameleon. Rabbit replied, "I think someone hit Chameleon with a big almond branch and tried to kill her. Let's run away, or we might be the next victims!" Each ran in a separate direction.

On the road, Chicken stopped Rabbit and asked, "What has happened? Why is Chameleon screaming, and what are you running from?"

"There is a huge tree that hits anyone who is near it," answered Rabbit. "That is what happened to Chameleon, and now nobody knows where she's gone." Chicken yelled, "This is a disaster!" Then she ran off to warn her friends to stay away from the almond tree.

Along the road, Chicken met Sheep. Chicken warned Sheep of the danger, and told him to be careful. "Don't even think of going to that field, because the almond tree that grows there kills and eats anyone who wanders near it."

Sheep swiftly ran to tell his friend Horse, saying, "There is grave danger in the field and the village. No one should leave their home today."

Horse ran to the other side of the farm, where Cow was grazing on the hill. "Did you hear what happened?"

"No, I didn't," replied Cow.

"Everyone is talking about it," said Horse. "The village, the farm, and the field are coming to an end. We are all in grave danger!"

When Cow ran off to look for a hiding place, she saw Turtle walking slowly along. Turtle said to Cow, "I want to tell you something important that happened to our friend Chameleon. She had an incident. Someone hit her on the head with a big branch."

"That is not important," said Cow, "but you must know that Judgment Day is coming, and the end of the world will follow. There will be disasters, and horrible things are going to happen to us all."

Having worked herself into a state of panic, Cow started to flee. A small peasant boy saw Cow running along, and thought she might be thirsty. The child caught Cow's rope and dragged her toward the well in the field.

At that very moment, Turtle, Chameleon, Rabbit, Chicken, Horse, and Sheep were walking by. They stopped to watch the small boy, saying, "That poor cow is going to be the first victim!

What a sad ending for her. We are all going to face the same destiny, because the end is near."

Their fear and astonishment grew as the boy and Cow reached the well. Cow refused to drink, so the boy let go of Cow's rope, and she wandered away. Then the boy drank from the well. After drinking, he lay down under the almond tree and fell asleep.

Cow went to her friends, and was greeted as a hero because she had come back safely. An hour passed while the animals stood watching. Suddenly, a small almond fell near the boy, who opened his eyes and smiled. He picked up the almond, washed it, and ate it. Then he slowly walked off toward the village.

Wide-eyed, with a look of relief, Chameleon said, "This boy is lucky. At least the almond did not fall on his head, as happened to me. But what good is being lucky now, when we are all going to die?"

Suddenly, a small bird passed over the field. It circled down and landed near the animals, saying, "I saw and heard everything from start to finish. You exaggerated the whole story. A small almond fell on Chameleon's head, and she turned it into a big deal. So don't believe everything you hear. And you should not be so hasty in your judgment."

"How do we know that what you're telling us is true?" asked Chameleon.

"The proof is that the boy was not harmed," replied the bird. "Now, goodbye. I am going to visit the well for myself."

The bird flew to the well and took a drink. He flitted from branch to branch, singing. The animals were so happy and relieved, they followed the bird to the well, shouting, "What a super bird! A smart bird!"

When the bird flew to his nest in the neighboring field, all of the birds were waiting to congratulate him. Because he had demonstrated such wisdom, they appointed him to be their leader, and king of the field. All the animals in that field respected and feared him. The birds wanted to know how he had been able to become so powerful, even though he was small in size.

From that day on, all the birds have called him Super Bird. Whenever they see a dangerous hawk or eagle flying above them, they are afraid, and seek protection from Super Bird. Each time this happens, the heroic Super Bird says to himself, "I hope Eagle and Hawk heard the stories that everyone is telling about my heroic feat, and not what really happened."

Plants

The Story of the Baatharan Shrub

(Artemisia judaica)

- EGYPT -

(A SOUTH SINAI BEDOUIN STORY)

Abou Salem[1] lived with his wife in a deep desert valley between the mountains. In the folds of this beautiful land, he worked long, hard days as a "coaler"—a person who makes coal.[2] Each day, he collected bundles of dry twigs from the trees growing nearby. He mounded the twigs just right, covered them

---

1. In Arab culture, people are known by the name of their eldest son. *Abou Salem* means "Father of Salem." *Om Salem* means "Mother of Salem."
2. "Coal," as used here, refers to charcoal.

with earth, and lit them to create a slow-burning fire that formed the coal.

By making the coal and selling it in the marketplace, Abou Salem was able to earn an income that provided all of the things his family needed to live. He was also doing something good for the trees. Cutting the dry parts, which were hindering their growth, brought new life to the branches.

Om Salem, who was Abou Salem's wife, was a herder. She also had to do all of the household chores, because Abou Salem's work required him to stay away from home for as long as a week to ten days at a time, camping out in the valley until he had collected the wood needed to produce the coal. Only then would Abou Salem return home.

Once, when Abou Salem was out in the valley collecting wood, his infant son became so sick that he began to vomit and have diarrhea. Om Salem searched for a cure for her son in that hot, dry land, where there was so little water that nothing grew except the desert plants. Bedouins often use plants for medicine. They sometimes discover the healing properties of certain plants by observing which plants camels are eating to cure themselves of particular ailments.

Om Salem walked slowly through the desert and identified the plants growing nearby. For some time, she did not find any useful plants. At last, she discovered a small stand of the baatharan shrub.

"Why don't I prepare a concoction made from this plant, and give it to Salem?" she asked herself. "Perhaps it could cure him?"

Salem was growing more seriously ill with each passing hour. Om Salem was extremely distressed, and afraid that if something was not done soon to cure her son, he would die.

Working as quickly as she could, Om Salem made a solution from the baatharan plant. She placed a handful of ground leaves, stems, and flowers into a small piece of clean cloth, and tied it closed at the top. Then she boiled a pot of water and poured the steaming water into a cup. After lowering the cloth containing parts of the baatharan shrub into the hot water, Om Salem covered the cup and allowed the solution to steep for about an hour— until the essence of the plant had entered the water.

When the medicine was ready, Om Salem took a few drops of the baatharan solution and placed them into her son's mouth. She did this several times over the course of the day, sitting next to

Salem for many hours, watching as his face grew more sickly and pale. "I hope this plant will cure my son," she prayed.

Time passed slowly. Om Salem noticed that the color was beginning to return to her son's face. He moaned, and his body stirred. Slowly, slowly, his health started to improve. When at last he turned his head and reached for his mother's milk, Om Salem lifted him gently to her breast. Tears ran down her cheeks as she sat and watched Salem feed. In the coming days, Salem's health came back to him, until he was well again.

When her husband returned, Om Salem told him of what had happened to their son, and what she had done to cure him. "Thanks to Allah[3] that he was able to recover by using the baatharan plant!" he exclaimed.

After Salem was fully cured, Abou and Om Salem began to tell others about how the baatharan plant could be used to cure stomach ailments, vomiting, and diarrhea. Over time, other healers discovered that the baatharan plant could help to cure other ailments, like indigestion. They found that baatharan would get rid of stomach worms, and that it could be used for storing and preserving woolen clothes during the summer heat.

3. The Muslim name for God.

From that day forward, the healing powers of baatharan became well known. This healing desert plant is now widely used by the Bedouin of Sinai.

To another plant story in another time, inshallah (God willing).

Baatharan shrub *(Artemisia judaica)*
(Photo by Dr. Elaine Solowey)

Qours Annee and the Rat

– LEBANON –

A farmer was out collecting wood from the forest. He gathered a little firewood every day, even during the heat of summer, so that he would be prepared when winter's cold winds began to blow.

One day, while on his way to the forest, the farmer saw something that caused him to stop and watch. A very busy rat was coming and going, eating from a certain plant, but not from the other plants that grew nearby.

"What plant could that be?" the farmer wondered. "And why is the rat eating only that kind of plant?"

The farmer was so intrigued by the rat's activities that he hid behind the bushes and stayed to observe. He counted the number of times that the rat was pacing along its trail, and discovered that it was passing by more than three times an hour. As his curiosity grew, the farmer left his hiding place, and quietly sneaked along the trail behind the rat as it moved.

Wawo! What the farmer found was far more impressive than the number of trips the rat was taking. It was feeding on a dead poisonous snake. Each time the rat ate some of the snake, he made his way back along the trail, and had another course of his meal from that specific plant.

"Why is this happening?" thought the farmer. "What is behind this strange lunch, and why is the rat doing things this way?"

The farmer imagined another way to help him solve this puzzle. He waited until the rat left the place where the plant grew, and watched the rat walk down the trail to eat from the snake. Then the farmer pulled the plant out of the ground and hid again.

The rat came back to eat from the plant, but could not find it. It searched and searched, but saw nothing growing around where the plant had been—not a single leaf…nothing.

Each time the rat circled the place where the plant had grown, it became more and more frantic, until finally, it seemed to be going mad. Soon, the rat grew weaker, but still it kept searching all over for a similar plant to eat.

While he was watching the rat's desperate attempt to find the plant, the farmer's mind was working furiously to uncover the plant's secret. He was extremely upset because of what was happening to the rat, so he spread some of the plant's leaves around the place where the rat had been eating. But it was too late. The rat had become poisoned from eating the snake. The farmer watched, helpless, as the rat fell over, kicked a few times, and died.

The farmer did not move. He sat quietly for a long time, and contemplated all that he had witnessed. Then he asked himself a most important question: "Why did the rat die soon after it no longer had the plant to eat?"

At last, the farmer's eyes opened wide as he understood what he had seen. He got up and raised his arms toward the sky. He was confident that this rat had been consuming a poisonous snake and curing itself by eating from the plant called *qours annee.*[1]

1. Field eryngo *(Eryngium creticum)* is a common plant used to treat snakebites. The Arabic name, qours annee, which means "sting from me," refers to the use of field eryngo to treat scorpion stings.

The farmer knew that his discovery could save many lives. He was so excited that he told everyone he met about the snake, the rat, and the plant. The news spread far and wide. Qours annee is now famous as a nutritious wild edible plant, and as an antidote to the venom found in snakebites.

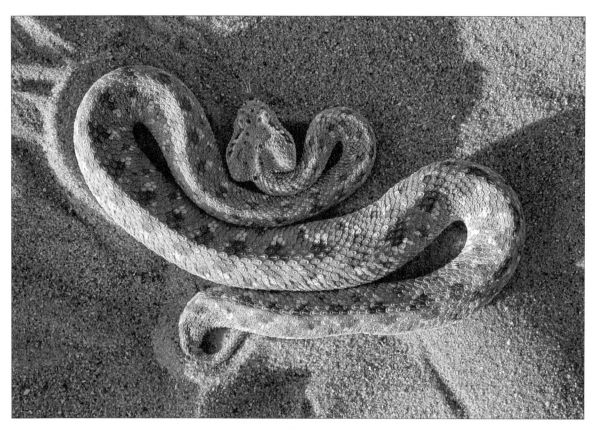

Persian horned viper *(Pseudocerastes persicus)*
(Photo by Elad Topel)

The Tree of a Life

- ISRAEL -

A TU B'SHEVAT TALE[1]

There came a time when the rains failed, and the soil was as dry as desert bones. Wells were empty, and animals wandered far to find life-giving water. Crops withered. Food was scarce, and hunger's knobby fingers gripped the land.

People went to Honi, the Circle Maker. They knew that he had a special way of praying. "Only you can bring the rain," they said. "Please do something before we all perish!"

Honi nodded his head gravely. Then he wandered off into the desert, where he etched a circle in the sand. Stepping into the

---

1. *Tu B'Shevat*, the Jewish "New Year for Trees," marks the time when trees awaken from their winter sleep in Israel. It is celebrated on the fifteenth (*Tu*) day of *Shevat*, which is the eleventh month of the Hebrew calendar.

37

center, Honi started speaking to God, asking for rain to quench the thirst of the people, the plants, and the animals.

For many days, Honi prayed. He sat in the prayer circle while the sun beat down on his head. At night, the stars kept him company beneath the cold dome of desert dark.

At last, a fine drizzle began to fall. "What is this?" cried Honi as he looked up toward the sky. Then he said to God, "Please send us some generous rain; enough rain to water this dusty land and slake the thirst of the people and the Earth."

Heavy rain began to fall with the sound of a million tiny drums. At first, it splashed up puffs of dust. Brown ribbons of water began to flow across the land, filling the wadis[1] with streams of mud. Rivers overflowed their banks and flooded the villages. People climbed up to the temples on high ground.

"Stop the rain!" they called out to Honi. "We only wanted enough rain so we would be able to live, not so much that we would need to build an ark, like our forefather Noah!"

Honi stepped back into the circle and raised his arms to Heaven. The rain stopped falling.

As the days went by, flowers bloomed in the desert, and trees

---

1. *Wadi* is the common term for "valley" in the lands of the Bedouin.

sprouted new shoots and leaves. The land turned green and rich with life.

Everywhere he went, people turned to Honi and said, "*Rav todot*—thank you very much."

As he often did after days of prayer, Honi began to wander.

One day at sunrise, he saw a young farmer planting a carob tree. "*Boker tov,*" said Honi.

"*Boker tov,*" replied the farmer.

"How long before you will be able to pick fruit from the branches of that tree?" asked Honi.

"This tree will not feed the likes of us," the farmer replied. "Its first fruit will be picked by the hands of my grandchildren, some seventy years hence."

"You are a patient man," said Honi.

"Patience feeds the roots of the family tree," said the farmer. "I now eat the fruit from trees planted by my own grandfather when he was a young man."

Honi continued along the path. He climbed a hilltop that looked out over a green valley, rich with new growth that had sprouted after the rains. Seeking shade in the shadow of a large

rock, Honi took pleasure in seeing what the rains had brought. Overcome at last by the long journey, Honi found that his head was beginning to droop, and soon, his eyes closed. He fell into a long, deep sleep that was rich with dreams.

Time passed. Honi's eyelids fluttered open. He yawned and stretched. "What a wonderful rest," Honi thought to himself as he stood and looked around. Full of energy, Honi walked back down the path toward home.

"Something has changed," he said aloud. "The world looks different."

In time, Honi again passed the farmer's land. He saw a different farmer picking carob pods from a magnificent old tree.

"*Shalom*," said Honi.

"*Shalom*," responded the farmer, as he continued to pick the carob pods.

"This tree…" asked Honi, "…I am confused. Is my mind still caught in a dream? This tree seems to be growing in the same place where I saw a farmer planting a sapling a short time ago."

"That is impossible," said the farmer. "This tree was planted by my grandfather many years past."

Honi stumbled back on his heels in fear and wonder, barely catching himself with his staff. It was then that he realized he had slept his life away while the world had borne fruit around him. He understood, at last, that the purpose of life was to plant and prepare the way for future generations to flourish.

Friendship

The Camel Who Saved Its Master

- EGYPT -

(A STORY FROM THE ABABDA TRIBE
OF SOUTH/CENTRAL EGYPT. RED SEA)

Nugros was a camel breeder who lived in a wadi near Sikait. In that land, long ago, the Romans mined emeralds from a nearby quarry and worshipped in a large, ornate temple. The valley was so well sheltered by the mountains that passersby along the closest road, which connected Hurghada to Shalateen, would not suspect that people lived in that lonely, arid place.

While Nugros was growing up, his father had often brought camels back from his long journeys to the market in Shalateen.

He showed Nugros how to train camels and teach them to obey his every command. Every few years, they crossed the border and went to one of the largest camel markets in the Sudan.

After one successful trip to the camel market, Nugros brought a special camel back to his valley near Sikait. As soon as he started to train this camel, Nugros grew excited, because he could see that it was an intelligent animal with a lot of spirit. He quickly grew fond of this camel, whom he named *Olouban*, which means "playful."

Nugros talked to his camel and looked it carefully in the eyes. He fed and groomed it well, but sometimes, Nugros would be rough on the camel as he worked to teach it in the ways his father had shown him. At the beginning of the training, in order to prove who was master, Nugros performed a special maneuver: he put his arms around Olouban's neck and flipped him onto the ground.

Even though his training techniques were strict, Nugros and his camels were very close, and shared a mutual respect. Nugros would ride Olouban into the wadi to search for new sources of water in springs and wells. Together, they looked for unique trees, like the arak[1], which the Ababda people use to clean their teeth.

---

1. The frayed twig or root of the shrubby arak tree *(Salvadora persica)* is known as *miswak*. It is soaked in rosewater, chewed until fibrous, and used as a toothbrush to clean the teeth and gums. Miswak kills harmful bacteria and prevents the buildup of plaque. Rosewater sweetens the breath and helps with digestion.

Sometimes they would discover other trees, like the heglig[2], which has fruit that helps people who are diabetic.

Branch of the heglig tree *(Balanites aegyptiaca),* with fruit on the ground.
(Photo by Dr. Elaine Solowey)

2. The heglig tree, *Balanites aegyptiaca,* has long been known for its use in medicine. The fruit pulp is used to treat diabetes. Root extracts have been used to treat malaria, edema, and stomach upset. An infusion made from the bark eases heartburn, and is also used for de-worming cattle.

When no one was riding Olouban, he would sit on the ground and rub himself against the sand to cool down. Like other camels, when Olouban was bored, he would regurgitate his food and start chewing it again.

Nugros and Olouban were true friends. Nugros often bothered Olouban, and teased him by poking twigs in his back.

One day, as the two friends were strolling in the wadi looking for plants and rocks, some dark clouds started to form. Nugros was happy, because clouds meant rain—and the life-giving water that would grow more plants.

Soon, it started to rain. Nugros decided to head back home to his village, which was built on a hilltop so it wouldn't wash away when sudden rains came, which often turned into flash floods.

The rain started coming down fast. Though camels are excellent desert riders, the rain-soaked sand was making Olouban's footing uncertain, and Nugros' ride became wobbly. Afraid of falling off the camel, Nugros decided to dismount and continue running toward home. Olouban also started running, but the rains were getting harder and heavier.

In a short while, the water rose so high that Nugros and Olouban had to start swimming. Nugros was struggling to swim, and was becoming afraid. They were both being carried swiftly downstream by the rushing waters, and were crashing into trees.

Time after time, Nugros was nearly lost beneath the roiling waters, but whenever a muddy wave forced his head beneath the surface, Nugros clung for his life to Olouban's neck, and was able to come up for air. Olouban's steadfast swimming kept his friend from drowning.

When a giant wave tore them loose from one another, Nugros screamed, "Olouban, boy, swim this way. You have to catch up with me, so we can make it home!" But the strong current pushed them farther apart. Eventually, they separated, and Nugros watched helplessly as Olouban was carried downstream.

Even though Nugros was heartbroken at the loss of his friend, he tried to collect his emotions and regain his focus so he could swim toward the side of the wadi where the mountains were higher and save himself. After some time, he was able to pull himself up onto higher ground, and out of the torrent that raged down through the valley. He hiked along the ridges of the high mountains for a long time, calling "Oloubon, Oloubon!" over and over again, until his voice was hoarse. Nugros finally saw his village in the distance, but seeing his home only made him feel even more empty. Without his friend Olouban at his side, he felt weary and alone.

When Nugros arrived in the village, everyone was relieved to see him. His family and friends ran over and embraced him. They had worried that he had drowned in the flood. "No, I am here, and safe," said Nugros.

Trying to see that there was light even in the darkest moment, Nugros said, "And the rains will soon turn the valley lush and green."

Then someone looked all around and asked, "Where is Olouban? What happened to him?"

Nugros looked at that person, and tears welled up in his eyes. A lump rose in his throat, and he could not speak.

Days and weeks passed while Nugros looked far and wide for his camel, to no avail. Though Nugros was a skilled tracker, and could identify each individual camel from any village by its tracks, it seemed that Olouban had disappeared. Nugros started to accept that his dear friend Olouban was gone.

One day, after Nugros had finished his morning prayer, he walked slowly back toward his family's tent. As he looked off toward the horizon in the distance, the silhouette of a camel, loping along, appeared on the ridgeline. When the camel looked down at the village and saw Nugros, it turned and galloped toward him. After a long and arduous journey, Olouban had come home to his friend.

Camels will never forget.

(Photo by Dr. Anton Khalilieh)

Raji over the Rainbow

- JORDAN -

Raji was a young boy who lived with his mother and father in an old house at the far edge of the village on the banks of the Jordan River. He often went to fish and swim by himself, because no one lived in the house next door, and all of the other children lived too far away. Raji was bored spending time alone, and wished he could have friends or neighbors nearby to play with.

Because he was an only child, Raji's parents were devoted to him, and he received all their attention. As he grew, Raji became spoiled, and developed a bad habit of relentlessly asking for anything he wanted. This displeased his parents very much.

One day, Raji's mother sat him down and said, "Son, I have some very good news. I am going to have a baby. Soon, you will have a new brother or sister."

Raji was extremely happy when his brother, Rawi, was born. "Finally," he thought, "I have someone to play with!" Raji waited several months to share playtime with his new little brother, but Rawi was just too young to play with Raji.

In the eyes of a boy Raji's age, Rawi was growing very slowly. In time, Raji lost patience and said, desperately, "I am bored playing with my small brother. He doesn't walk or talk, he just flutters his hands like a bird, makes noises like a cat when he laughs, and annoys me with his crying, day and night."

One morning, Raji woke up to hear a strange noise close to the river. Raji jumped out of bed and ran to the balcony to see what was happening. He was overjoyed to find a big truck full of furniture parked in front of the house next door. Raji watched as workers moved the furniture inside. He was even more excited to see two boys and a girl playing in the yard.

"At long last," thought Raji, "I will have friends my own age to play with!" Raji washed his face, put on his clothes, and quickly went downstairs.

Walking into the new neighbor's yard, Raji stepped up to the children and said, "I am your neighbor. My name is Raji."

The older boy replied, "My name is Saber. This is my brother Samer and my sister Lina."

Raji said, "Welcome! Would you like to come over and play together in my house?" The children got permission from their mother and joined Raji.

At Raji's house, the children had great fun playing together. Raji shared all of his toys and favorite games. He was excited to have new friends, and wanted to share with them.

When they were done playing, Saber said to Raji, "Would you like to come over and play at our house tomorrow?" And so, Raji started going to the house of his new friends and playing with their toys.

For a time, Raji was content with his new friends. His parents were glad to see him spending time with other children. They were also relieved that Raji was not always pestering them with endless requests for new things.

Then Raji started to notice something that upset him. At first, because he liked his new friends, he did not want to believe what he was seeing, but he could not deny that it was true. Every time Raji's friends came to visit, they would grab one of his toys and take it away. After a while, Raji started to become annoyed. From then on, even when the children asked permission to play with Raji's toys or wanted to play in the garden nearby, he would say, "These toys are mine, and I am not going to allow you to play with them. And you can't come into my garden."

The children became angry. Finally, Saber said, "From now on, we are not going to allow you to play with our toys, either, and you will not be able to watch the pigeon bird tower that overlooks our house, or ride the horses in the barn."

Samer added, "We do not want to talk to you anymore." Then Lina exclaimed, "Let us go." And the children went home.

One day, as his neighbors were playing in their garden, Raji watched them from the small window of his room. They were having a great time chasing butterflies, running around the flowerbeds, and hiding behind trees. Raji stayed in his room playing alone, but he was not having any fun at all, so he started to feel bored again.

By himself, Raji went out to the backyard to play, but it was very quiet. Raji lifted his head to the sky and saw a fog spreading like a soft blanket across the river valley. Then an arching rainbow

began to shimmer with beautiful colors. To Raji, it seemed that the rainbow arose from a nearby field. Raji said, "I am sure I can reach the rainbow and touch it. That way, it will be all mine."

Raji went to the field and started chasing the rainbow. No matter how fast he ran, the rainbow stayed far away, and remained very high up. When the sun disappeared, the rainbow faded, and then it was gone.

When Raji returned home, his father asked, "Where were you?"

Raji replied, "I chased a rainbow and tried to catch it, but it disappeared."

His father laughed and said, "Rainbows are too high up for us to reach them. It is only the colors that we see."

Raji asked, "Where do rainbows come from?"

His father answered, "Rainbows form when the light of the sun passes through the rain or fog."

At that moment, the sun hid back behind the clouds, and rain started to fall. When the sun emerged and its rays shone through the rain, the rainbow appeared once more.

Raji screamed with delight. "Hurry, Father, take me with your car to the rainbow before it disappears again. I want to hide it in my room. Hurry!" But the rainbow grew farther and farther away, and then it disappeared when the rain stopped. Raji was sad and started complaining ceaselessly, as usual. "I want the rainbow, and I want its colors to play with!"

His father said, "Alright, then, get in the car and come with me. You will have a rainbow that will never disappear."

Raji exclaimed happily, "Is that true, Father? But how?"

"You will see in a short while!" said his father. "Be patient."

Raji's father parked the car near a bookstore, and Raji accompanied him inside. His father bought some big white paper and a box of crayons, and then drove Raji home.

On the paper, his father drew a big rainbow and colored it with beautiful hues: violet, indigo, blue, green, yellow, orange, and lastly, red.

Raji was fascinated and said, "That is an awesome rainbow. And it is all mine, right, Dad?"

His father nodded, and said, "Yes, it is all yours, and it will never disappear!"

Raji grabbed a pen and drew a man and a child over the rainbow. He turned to his father and said, "This is you and me, Dad, climbing over the rainbow and going with it on a journey far away."

His father asked, "Do you want to take anyone else with us?"

Raji answered, "Yes, we will take Mother and my brother, Rawi." As he drew them on the rainbow, Raji thought for a moment, and then asked, "Should we take the neighbors' children, also?"

His father answered, "If you wish."

Raji drew his three friends over the rainbow. Then he picked up the paper, saying, "I am going to show it to my friends."

Raji hurried to his friends' house and knocked on the door. When they let him in, Raji showed them the drawing, and said, "Look, this is my father, my mother, my brother, and you. I am going to take you with me on a trip over the rainbow, because you are my friends and we will play together."

Samer asked, "Did you draw this?"

Raji answered, "My father drew the rainbow, but I drew the rest, and I have many papers and crayons. Come with me, and we can draw together."

The neighbors' children looked at each other for a moment as if wondering what to do, but then they all smiled and joined Raji. Each of them drew a beautiful picture and presented it to the others. Raji was so happy that he said, "I am changed now, all thanks to the rainbow and its beautiful colors."

Ever since that day, Raji has shared with Saber, Lina, and Samer, and has never felt bored or lonely again. He often goes out with his friends to play along the Jordan River, to see and experience the amazing world of nature that God has provided us.

On certain days, when the sun comes out during a rainstorm, a rainbow rises from the field and arches over the river. "Look," says Raji, "the rainbow connects everything we see with a bridge of beautiful colors."

The Well of Judgment

- PALESTINE -

Long ago, when the animals could speak like human beings, there lived a pigeon, a donkey, and a sunbird. These three animals were best friends who liked and cared for one another in sickness and health.

One day, as they were walking along, they saw a vast, empty land. Sunbird became excited, and started to chatter.

"What a beautiful place!" she said. "Let us plant a garden and live here."

Her friends looked at her strangely and replied, "What are you saying? This land is not ours! We cannot take it from its owners."

Sunbird was embarrassed, but Pigeon took her side, saying, "We can ask around, and if we don't find the owners, then we can use the land."

Sunbird and Donkey liked this idea. They investigated and asked everyone they could find, but no one claimed the land. So they decided to plant a garden.

Sunbird wanted to plant sesame, but Donkey didn't eat sesame, and wanted to grow watermelon.

Sunbird and Donkey argued for a time, until Pigeon finally said, "We will plant wheat. We all like to eat wheat."

Before they could plant, however, the three friends had to walk around the field and clear away all the litter: the plastic cups and plates that people had thrown away.

"Who still uses plastic?" Pigeon asked.

"Don't they realize it's bad for the environment?" added Donkey.

After cleaning the land, they sowed the seeds of wheat. Each day, they walked out into the field to pull up the weeds and pick up the trash that people had dumped there. When the rains did not come, they watered the wheat field. Gradually, the wheat grew thick and high, and formed large heads of seeds that moved like waves when the wind blew. On some evenings, when the sun was low in the sky, Pigeon, Donkey, and Sunbird stood quietly at the edge of the field, watching how the wheat danced with the breeze and spoke with the soft voice of the wind.

One day, as they were tending the plants, Donkey said. "Look! The wheat has grown taller than me!"

"Yes, it has!" said Pigeon.

"Tomorrow morning, we can begin to harvest the wheat," said Sunbird.

It had taken a long time for the wheat to mature, and had required much hard work. Donkey, Pigeon, and Sunbird were very happy to see that their crop had ripened. They decided to come back early the next day to begin the harvest.

That night, the three friends were so excited they could hardly sleep. All of their patience and sweat were about to be rewarded. They met each other just before sunrise and walked together to the wheat field, but instead of finding a rich crop waiting to be harvested, they were shocked and dismayed to discover that all of the wheat had been eaten.

Sunbird turned to Donkey and said, "You did this!"

"No, NO! I didn't," answered Donkey, with hurt in his voice. "It must have been Pigeon and all of his hungry friends."

"It was not me," said Pigeon angrily. "That leaves Sunbird as the culprit."

Sunbird started crying, and then she said, "How can you blame me for stealing the wheat, after all we've been through together as friends?"

"Whoever it was that stole our wheat, we now have nothing left to eat," Pigeon lamented.

The three friends were confused, and they didn't know what to do, so they decided to ask the wise owl for her advice.

Owl listened to their story, and then she said, "Hear me, and you will know the innocent and the guilty. You should go to the deep well. Whoever passes over the well by walking the rope that is stretched across the opening will be innocent, but the one who stumbles and falls in is guilty."

Donkey complained, "I have small feet and thick hooves, and it will be hard for me to hold onto the rope."

"Indeed," said Owl. "However, the magical rope will only drag the *guilty* person down."

The three friends walked toward the well. Along the way, they decided that they would all try to walk across the magical rope, from the smallest to the biggest.

As Sunbird began to walk across, she said, "*Sousou* is my name. If I am guilty, then let me fall." Sunbird passed safely across the well.

Next came Pigeon. Though he wavered on the rope, Pigeon also made it across.

Donkey went last. As he was passing, the rope began to sway. Braying loudly, Donkey fell down, down, down into the well. He landed with a splash and started screaming. "I am sorry. Please forgive me. Save me!"

Sunbird and Pigeon looked at one another and wondered.

"Should we forgive him?" asked Sunbird.

"Of course we ought to forgive him," said Pigeon. "He is our friend."

Working together, Sunbird and Pigeon found a long rope and tied a big loop on the end. Then they lowered the rope down into the well, and Donkey slipped the loop around his waist. Using all of their strength, they pulled together and slowly raised Donkey out of the well.

Once Donkey was safely back on land, Sunbird and Pigeon asked him, "Why did you do it? What possessed you to eat all of our wheat? How could you do such a thing, after all our hard work and everything we've been through together?"

Donkey lowered his head and apologized again. His ears drooped. Tears slid down his face and landed in small puffs on the dry ground. "Please forgive me."

Pigeon and Sunbird walked over to their friend and wiped away his tears.

"Everybody makes mistakes sometimes," they said. "But we are still your friends, just like we were before."

Palestine sunbird *(Cinnyris osea)*
(Photo by Dr. Anton Khalilieh)

Stewardship

I Wonder Who It Will Be?

- PALESTINE -

There once was a little town on the shore of a small lake. In the lake, a school of beautiful and colorful fish lived in peace and harmony. The water was so clear and clean that the water creatures and sea plants believed that their home was a small piece of paradise.

One day, someone threw an empty can into the lake. Astonished, a group of fish gathered around to watch this strange object fall and land in their midst. It was a unique day, unlike any of the days that had come before it. The routine life of the lake dwellers was broken, and their quiet life disturbed.

As soon as the strange object touched the bottom, it created controversy among the inhabitants of the lake. One small fish pleasantly and playfully said, "Hurray, hurray! A gift from the other world." Looking around at the faces of the other fish, she asked, "Who sent this gift? It has strange colors, and I have never seen anything like it before."

Another fish replied, "I think that one of the creatures that lives on land has dropped it, and must be looking for it now."

Moments later, a big fish came to warn them, saying, "That object is not to be touched. It is a dangerous object that can harm you. Don't you know that the humans who live on the land are the ones who made this thing? They are the same creatures that throw their nets into the water to capture us. Don't be fooled into thinking that this is a gift."

The other fish slowly swam to the wise fish to hear more about this startling event. As they gathered, there was a moment of silence before the wise fish spoke again in a quiet voice. "Yes, the humans who live on the other side of our world are the ones doing this. I think this is a warning. If it happens again, it will bring disaster, and will endanger our lives. All of the water creatures will die."

The small fish laughed, and said, "What an exaggeration. What's wrong with receiving a gift from the other world? We

should examine it, and try to understand why it was made and what it is used for."

Another fish asked her to be silent, saying, "Who knows more than this wise fish?" When the meeting was finished, everyone went back to work.

The next day, they heard another large, strange object splash down into the waters. It penetrated the quiet of the lake, and almost struck one of the fish before settling on the bottom and stirring up a cloud of silt. At first, the fish became frightened, and scattered to find refuge; but when the waters calmed and cleared, the fish slowly gathered to make sure everyone was fine, and to examine the huge object that had come crashing into their world, almost killing them.

They saw how the object had ruined some of their beautiful sea life. It had crushed ancient, delicate coral and shells. After a few moments, the wise fish came to see the horrific scene. The fish were surprised to see the wise fish come out again, for she rarely left the home, where she spent her time pondering the matters of the lake. Everyone watched the face of the wise fish closely, and it showed signs of anger. They all waited in silence to hear what she was going to say, but were surprised when the wise fish swam away without saying a word. This was enough of a sign for everyone to realize that what had happened was a big event. Days passed, and this event was all that anyone talked about.

One morning, someone shouted, "Hide! A big net is coming our way!" Everyone swam away, and hid as fast as they could.

After the net disappeared, they gathered to make sure that everyone was accounted for, and then they congratulated each other for surviving. One angry fish said, "What's wrong with this human? He destroys the things that give him life and sustenance. In the past, the lake was deeper, but now, the depth is barely a few meters. The water was cleaner, and there were more inhabitants among us—but now, our life here is intolerable."

In the silence that followed, a sense of sadness and insecurity settled over the inhabitants of the lake. The fish glanced around at one another, waiting for someone to tell them what they should do, but no one spoke.

At that moment, a low, soothing voice arose from the waters. In spite of the fearful mood that had been cast over the other fish, the wise fish started singing this song:

I dreamt last night that someone who wants to make life beautiful
  will sing a song of hope.

I had a dream that tomorrow will bring a wise man
  to repair what his fellow men destroyed.

He is going to sing like me, and will be hope for us all—
  for the people and for all life.

Others will join in his singing.

I wonder who it will be?

Thanking God for All Things

- EGYPT -

(A SOUTH SINAI BEDOUIN STORY)

A long time ago, there was a man who lived with his mother and his wife. They had a small farm down in a valley between the mountains. The man was a herder, known for taking good care of his sheep and camels. His mother shared the work by helping him raise the young animals.

Time passed, and the man and his wife were blessed with many children; but the husband's mother was growing old, and found that she could no longer care for the sheep and camels.

In time, the old woman needed someone's help just to move about the house.

The herder worked hard, and was the breadwinner of the family. His wife stayed at home and took care of the growing household. As time passed, she became unhappy because her mother-in-law could not move about on her own or help around the house, and had to be assisted in everything she did.

One day, the herder's wife said to her husband, "It's going to be either me or your mother in this house."

Her husband asked, "What on earth has happened for you to speak of my mother this way?"

She replied, "Your mother is old, and has become a nuisance. Her needs are now greater than the needs of our children. I'm tired of the situation at home—having to take care of the children and your mother—and on top of that, the sheep. So you have to make a choice: it's either me or your mother in this house."

The husband was stuck, and didn't know what to do with his wife's ultimatum. He thought and thought about his dilemma. Finally, he chose to take his mother to a faraway place. Without telling her his plan, the herder helped his mother pack her belongings. Then, together, they rode on the back of a camel to a place near a spring. In that lonely place, far from other people, he struck up a fire on a large piece of tree bark, and left her enough food to feed herself.

When night was falling and the shadow of darkness crept across the land, his mother drifted off into a deep sleep, and the man quietly slipped away. He left his mother in that remote place between the mountains, and returned to his wife.

On the morning of the next day, when the mother woke up and started to feel around, she saw a strange man next to her who was wearing a white *galabiya* (Arab robe). Then a very strong wind started to blow, and cold weather came upon her in the place between the mountains. The water in the spring started to freeze. The old woman began to pray, and asked God to help her. She also counted her blessings, and thanked God for all that He had given to her.

On the third day, a different man appeared who looked similar to the man who had come to her on the first day. This time, the water in the spring started to boil from the heat. Praying, she thanked God, and hoped that all would be well.

After seven days had passed, the two men came to the old woman and asked, "Don't you know who we are?"

The old woman replied, "No, I don't know you."

Then the man who had appeared on the first day told her, "I am Winter, and I'm the one who came to you when the water turned to ice."

The other man said, "When I came to you, the water started boiling from my heat. I am Summer."

"You must be as you say," replied the old woman.

"Yes," said the first man.

Both men said to her, "You are a woman who is patient and thankful for all. For this reason, we will make you young again." As they rubbed their hands over her, a strange warmth spread throughout her body, and she began to change. Gradually, the woman was transformed, until she appeared as she had been when she was in her early twenties—youthful and beautiful. Her eyes were clear, her skin radiant, and her long black hair shone in the sun.

After the husband returned home and some days had passed, he said to his wife, "I need to visit my mother to see if she is still alive, and find out what has happened to her."

When the man entered the pass between the mountains, he went to the place where he had left his mother, near the eye of the spring. In place of his elderly mother, he found a lovely young woman. He asked the girl, "Have you seen an old woman nearby?"

The young woman replied, "I am your mother."

Stepping quickly back in surprise and shock, the herder said with a trembling voice, "I…I…don't believe you."

The young woman told him the story of what had happened to her, and then she answered all of his questions. After a time, the herder became convinced that she was telling the truth—that this was, indeed, his mother.

The herder took the young woman back home. When his wife saw the young woman come through the door of their house, she grew jealous and angry.

"Do not be angry," said her husband. "This is my mother."

"What kind of a tale is that? I don't believe you!" screamed his wife.

The herder asked his wife to sit down, and he told her the same story his mother had told him.

A disturbing expression of desire came over his wife's face, and then she demanded of her husband, "Take me to this place in the mountains where you left your mother." Since he knew his wife would not be happy until he did as she asked, the herder led his wife to that place in the mountains, and left her there.

His wife didn't thank her God, Allah, and she didn't pray to him. After seven days had passed, the two men came, Winter and Summer. They introduced themselves to her, and rubbed their hands upon her. Instead of growing young, however, the wife's skin became deeply wrinkled and spotted, her back stooped, and her eyes clouded. Her long dark hair turned white.

When her husband returned to the mountains to find her, he saw an ancient, haggard old woman.

"Who are you?" he asked. "And what have you done with my wife?"

His wife pleaded with him, saying, "Husband, it is me. I'm your wife. Please believe me!"

Her husband didn't believe her until she told him the entire story. When she returned home again, her children were so afraid of her that they cried and ran away. They could not recognize her as their mother, and did not want to be around this strange old woman.

Thus is the fate of those who refuse to care for their elders, and do not thank God for their blessings.

(Photo by Michael J. Caduto)

Iman's Journey

- JORDAN -

Iman and her family were invited to spend the day at a friend's farm. She was excited to go, because she loved to ride horses, and was an expert rider. Whenever Iman went horseback riding with her brother, Mohammed, their parents cheered them on as they raced by on horseback, saying, "Go, Iman! Go, Mohammed!"

"Your children ride very well," said her father's friend.

"Yes, we are very proud of them," Iman's father replied. "Soon, we will teach our youngest son, Yousef, to ride, as well. It's very important for our children to learn all types of sports. Our Prophet Mohammed, peace be upon him, encouraged Muslims to educate their children well and to teach them sports."

"You are absolutely right," replied her father's friend. "I have noticed you teach Iman everything that you teach her brother."

"Of course," answered Iman's father. "Islam teaches us to treat our children equally. We must love and support our daughters as we love and support our sons. The Prophet Mohammed, peace be upon him, encouraged Muslims to be fair with their children."

"Peace be upon him, he is a great example to follow," agreed the friend.

"Lunchtime!" called the friend's wife from up at the house. "Everyone, come in to eat."

"*Bism Allah*," everyone said as they began to eat, "in the name of God." Everyone acknowledged Allah except for Yousef, who forgot.

"Yousef," said Iman, "You must say 'in the name of God' before you eat, and say 'thanks to God' after you finish. Food is a gift from God, and we must always thank Him."

"In the name of God," Yousef said as he began to eat.

After eating their lunch, Iman, Mohammed, and their friends rode the horses out again. They were eager to explore their surroundings, to have an adventure, and to discover the natural world around the farm. Iman loved to watch the edge of the marsh for the yellow wagtail and its bright golden feathers. One of the children's favorite pastimes was to search for ripe seedpods hanging from the carob tree, and to eat some of the sweetly-scented beans with their chocolatey flavor.

While enjoying their outing, the children suddenly heard someone screaming in the distance. It sounded like the voice of a child. Iman stopped her horse and asked, wide-eyed, "Did you hear that?"

"Someone sounds like he is in trouble," her brother cried.

"AAAGGGHHH!" the young voice yelled again. This time, Iman did not wait for an explanation. "Go!" she instructed her horse, who galloped away so fast that the other riders could not keep up.

"Iman, wait for us!" She could hear them yelling behind her, but could not hesitate for fear that someone was in trouble.

Iman finally slowed down when she heard the screams getting closer. She jumped off her horse and strode toward a group of children she recognized as bullies and thugs from her school. The kids were throwing sticks and stones at a young boy. He looked very frightened, and he was hurt.

"What are you doing?" asked Iman, in a firm voice.

"Come join us," said the boy who seemed to be the leader of the mean gang.

"Grab some stones and throw them at Majed."

"Why?" Iman asked angrily.

"Because he looks different," the boy replied. Then the kids again started to throw sticks and stones at Majed. Some of them also threw stones at the trees, and at the birds that were perching on the branches overhead.

"Stop!" Iman yelled as she walked toward little Majed, and stood beside him.

"It is not right to pick on Majed just because he looks different. You should leave him alone. And you are destroying the peace in this lovely area."

"Oh, yeah? Then make us stop!" The gang leader mocked her as he ran to the nearest tree and pulled on a rope. A big net fell down and trapped Iman and Majed, who started to cry even harder.

"Ha! Ha! Ha!" the kids laughed.

"I think it's time for us to use our special stones, to cut the trees and hunt for birds," suggested the leader. "And don't worry about those two," he said, pointing his finger at Iman and Majed.

"They won't be going anywhere." Then he ran off into the field, and the rest of the mean kids followed.

"Don't be afraid, Majed. We will be alright," Iman reassured him.

Iman knew what she must do. Whenever there was trouble, she ran to the strongest power in the world...the power of God. Iman removed the pink scarf from around her neck, wrapped it around her head, and began to think about how she could get them out of this trouble spot.

Iman suddenly felt her arms become super-powerful. She held the net with both hands, and tore it in half.

"Wow," exclaimed Majed, "You're strong! How did you do that?"

Iman freed them both from the net. Then she took Majed by the hand, and they hid behind the nearest tree.

"We will wait for those nasty kids to get back, and then we will surprise them," she said. "But you must stay behind the tree until I call you. This tree will cover you."

A few minutes later, they heard the gang of kids returning.

"Huh?" exclaimed the gang leader in amazement as he saw the shredded net. "Where did they go?" he yelled.

"Are you looking for me?" asked Iman, stepping out from behind the tree with a big grin on her face.

"You can't get away from us. Attack her!" screamed the leader to the rest of the gang. The kids rubbed their stones together and threw them at Iman. As the stones flew through the air, they changed into fireballs.

Iman held up her beautiful pendant, which had *Allah* written on the front. Then she said, "In the name of God." Suddenly, the pendant turned into a shield. Iman held it to block the firestones from hitting her. Every firestone that struck her shield turned into coal and crumbled to the ground.

The gang leader started to panic. He quickly yelled to the others, "Charge!" The kids ran toward Iman to fight her, but they did not suspect that Iman's faith and prayer to God had given her superpowers, and that nature was protecting her. One by one, she fought them off.

While defending herself from the gang, she heard Majed yell, "Iman! Watch out!" She turned around and looked at the gang leader. He was rushing toward her with another net in which to trap her. Iman grabbed the net from him. She spun around and captured all of the gang members inside the net.

At last, Majed stepped out from behind the tree and stood next to Iman.

"Get me out," cried the gang leader. "Please let us all out. If you do, we will stop hurting you, and will not harm the trees or birds. We promise to treat little Majed well."

Iman then said to them all, "A true Muslim believes we are all created by one God, even trees, birds, and animals. Now you can all feel what it is like to be caught inside the net. We must try to live peacefully with one another and take care of the environment that surrounds us, and the nature we need to breathe, eat, and live."

The young people were amazed at the powerful teachings of Islam. Iman could now see regret in their eyes—regret over what they had done to her and especially to Majed, and the birds and the trees.

Iman continued, "You are lucky that God is so forgiving, especially when we admit our mistakes."

The members of the gang twisted in the net and looked around at each other, then gazed at Iman. They started to thank God, and promised not to hurt anyone, especially little children, animals, and birds. Only then did Iman tear the net in half to release the children, who cheered for their freedom.

Then the children turned around and went to a hidden place where they had been holding little birds in a net. They freed those birds, which flew up and escaped to the sky, singing songs of joy and freedom.

Iman led Majed over to her horse and helped him to mount into the saddle. "Show me the way to your house," she said. Majed pointed her down a narrow trail.

Once they reached Majed's house, Iman helped him to get down off the horse.

"Thank you very much for saving me today," said Majed. "You are really amazing."

"So are you, Majed, and don't let anyone tell you anything else."

Iman began to ride off, then turned and waved, saying, "Goodbye, my little friend."

As the sun was setting, Iman arrived at the farmhouse just in time to join her family for dinner.

Yellow wagtail *(Motacilla flava)*
(Photo by Dr. Anton Khalilieh)

Saving the Cedars of Lebanon

An Environmental Success Story
Shouf Biosphere Reserve

- LEBANON -

For thousands of years, stories of gigantic evergreen trees have been told around the cooking fire. Picture the majesty of an ancient Cedar of God tree, whose glowing branches have spread overhead for more than 3,000 years while stories have come to life in the imaginations of generations of children. Which events in human history have been witnessed by its green branches and wizened trunk? How many storms, fires, droughts, diseases, and times of war and peace has it survived?

Wood from the ancestors of today's cedars of Lebanon helped build the great temple of Solomon nearly 3,000 years ago. These legendary trees are symbols of strength and abundance in *The Epic of Gilgamesh,* and their roots and shoots spin a web of story and legend throughout the history of Lebanon.

There came a time, however, just decades ago, when the ancient forests where the cedars of Lebanon grow were in great danger of extinction. For thousands of years, trees had been cut and forests cleared to harvest wood for many uses, especially for building, firewood, cooking, and fuel. Forest fires burned down many venerable trees that had been growing since time out of mind.

Those who loved these beautiful trees fought incredible odds to save them from destruction. Fortunately, in the 1960s, the Lebanese government began the Project for the Improvement of the Lebanese Mountains.

When Lebanon's civil war erupted in 1975, people again cut down many trees, using the wood for cooking and heat as they tried to survive the extreme hunger and cold weather. The fighting also hindered plans to care for new cedar seedlings.

In time, people saw that in order to save the trees, the land first had to be preserved, and the habitat improved and irrigated

with water. Then the trees had to be replanted to grow new forests. When the Ministry of Agriculture in Lebanon realized that the cedars would not survive unless their habitat was conserved, they created the Green Plan. Villagers from around the Al Shouf Cedar Nature Reserve planted cedars to recreate a Lebanon that would be greener and more lush.

Cedar trees were planted in rows on hillside terraces, but many seedlings died long before they could become mature trees. In some cases, as many as half of the seedlings perished. Fortunately, some of the trees survived and became symbols of hope—living examples of how people can work together to cherish nature. Today, these spectacular trees can be seen in the rows of cedars of Lebanon that crown the hills of the Shouf Mountains.

These cedar forests dot the landscape and hillsides, weaving a living tapestry along with the older stands of cedar trees around Maasser, Barouk, and Ain Zhalta. As the young trees grow, they will one day express the wise old character of the ancient cedars, with magical, leaning shapes sculpted by wind, rain, and snow. This will only come to pass if the cedars live long enough to grow into their fantastical forms.

It takes time, money, hard work, and love to grow a forest, especially a stand of slow-growing trees like the cedars of Lebanon. Seedlings need a lot of care and attention if they are to survive. Foresters—people who grow trees and manage forests—know what needs to be done for each kind of tree. They know that planting a tree is more than just putting seedlings into the soil; trees need to be taken care of long after they have started to put down roots. *Rebuilding a green countryside is much more challenging than tearing it down.*

Saving a forest also takes leaders who care about saving the trees. The first plantings of cedars of Lebanon were supported by Kamal Joumblatt, a leader of the Druze community and a powerful force for conservation in the Shouf. In addition to expressing concern for the state of the forests of Lebanon, it is also said that he spent time in solitude, meditating by the famous La Martine cedar tree in Maasser Cedar Forest.

Kamal Joumblatt's work is being continued by his son, Walid Joumblatt, and by his son's wife Nora, both of whom support the Shouf Biosphere Reserve through their work with the Al-Shouf Cedar Society. Though the Al-Shouf Cedar Nature Reserve is under the care of the Lebanon Ministry of Environment, it is local people of all ages who continue the work started generations ago to save the cedars of Lebanon. Cedar-planting campaigns are now taking place all across Lebanon. The ancient story of the cedars of Lebanon has become a living legend, and the future of that story is in everyone's hands.

Cedar of Lebanon *(Cedrus libani)*. Having grown some 3,000 years, this is the oldest cedar tree in Lebanon's Shouf Cedar Reserve.
(Photo copyright Shouf Cedar Reserve: shoufcedar.org)

Wisdom

Salma and Her Little Bird

- JORDAN -

Salma lived with her grandmother in the little village of Rasoon on the slopes of the Ajloun Mountains in northern Jordan. She often went outside and walked through her family's garden, surrounded by the colors and scents of flowers and the bright flash of butterfly wings. When she opened her hand and offered some pistachios to the Persian squirrel who lived in a nearby oak tree, it came and ate from her palm.

Through the eyes of a ten year old fresh with wonder, Salma saw the sun lighten the sky of each new day. When she opened the window, Salma loved to hear the music of a special singing bird greet the dawn.

The fresh scent of thyme and daffodils blew in on the morning breeze, mingling with the aroma of her grandmother's fresh bread. In her innocence, Salma looked out across the valley and admired the clear Safi water that flowed through her village.

"Oh, how nice your fresh bread smells, Grandmother," Salma said.

By the time Salma left to play with the neighbors' children at around noon, the sun had filled the sky with its golden warmth. On her way to play with the girls, Salma collected flowers for her grandmother, who liked to decorate her vase with unique colors.

While she was playing, Salma noticed a little bird on the ground that was trying to fly. The bird was very tired, scared, and lonely. Salma approached the little bird and said softly, "Don't be afraid, I am not going to hurt you. What happened? Why are you so tired and miserable?"

The bird cried, "I was on a trip with the other birds and we were singing, filling up the air with our songs. Suddenly, a hunter shot me with his rifle and chased my friends away. I don't know where they are now, so I am alone, hurt, and sad."

Salma became upset as she listened to the story. Then she thought of a way to help the small bird. She picked it up and wrapped it in her jacket to keep it safe.

When Salma returned home, she greeted her grandmother, Hamida, and showed her the bird swaddled in the jacket. "Please, Grandmother," asked Salma, "may I keep the bird at home until it gets better? Please?"

"What a beautiful bird," said her grandmother. "You can keep it until it starts to recover, but you will have to take care of it."

"I promise!" said Salma. "Will you show me what to do?"

Salma's grandmother reached into the cupboard and took out two small saucers, which she gave to Salma. "One saucer is for water, and the other for food. Keep the water fresh, and fill the other saucer with some fresh fruit and seeds for the bird to eat."

Indeed, Salma took good care of the bird, and spoke kindly to it. Sometimes, she sang songs for the bird. "Music will help to make you happy," she said. Day by day, the bird started to heal and feel better.

One morning, Salma awoke to hear the bird warbling from where it perched near her window, filling her room with beautiful song. She quickly got up and found that the bird had recovered, and was full of life and energy.

Salma thought, "I saved him from death and agony. Now I can build a small cage to keep him in." She spent many hours working on the bird's cage, creating a little house with towers that she thought the bird would find a lovely home to live in. It was decorated with beautiful wildflowers. Inside, she placed a swing, a water fountain, and some seeds.

As Salma was moving the bird into the cage, the bird asked her with amazement, "What are you doing? It is true that you saved me from the hunter and his rifle, but now you have sentenced me to jail inside a cage, and taken away my freedom? God created me to fly through the open sky, and to sing so everyone can hear my songs."

Salma responded, "But look at the cage—it is beautiful. You can eat and play there, and no one will hurt you. Come on inside."

The bird entered the cage, even though it appeared to its wild eyes like a dark cell. Soon, the bird began to feel depressed and unhappy. Days passed as Salma cleaned and decorated the cage with flowers, and added water and seeds.

One evening, as Salma and her grandmother were eating dinner, she asked, "Why doesn't my bird sing anymore?"

Her grandmother laughed and answered, "My dear, the cage is small. Although it looks nice from the outside, from the inside, it

appears dark and gloomy. Would you like it if you were not allowed to play here and there in the village? Would you be comfortable living in a castle, but not having friends and family around?"

Salma wondered about what her grandmother had said. Then she replied, "Of course not, Grandmother. I love you, and I would not allow our little house to turn into a big castle where I would live without you."

Salma's grandmother didn't reply. She simply reached across the table, took Salma's hand gently in her own, and smiled.

"Now I understand," said Salma. "I did save my bird from the hunter, but then I locked him in a cage that appears to him like a prison. Without his friends, my bird is lonely."

Salma went to her room and peeked in at the little bird. Her heart felt for him. She decided to free the bird the next morning, so he could join his friends. Then she went to sleep.

In the morning, Salma got out of bed and opened the window. She placed the cage on the windowsill and opened the door. "It's time for you to leave and search for your friends," she said. The bird was so happy that it left the cage and flew high into the sky, singing a song of joy.

Days passed. Salma started to feel sad because she was alone in her room. She knew in her heart that it was right for her to have set the bird free, but she missed its company, and the sweet music that had greeted her with the sunrise.

Then, one morning, Salma opened her eyes and jumped out of bed to the sound of birds chirping and singing and pecking on her window. She opened the window to find a flock of birds fluttering around, happy and free. What a lovely sound it was, and what a beautiful sight to see the birds flying and singing.

While Salma admired the scene, one of the birds approached the window and said, "I am the bird you saved from death."

Salma replied, "Yes, and I learned that you cannot be happy living in a cage."

The bird replied, "What you say is true, my friend. You released me and gave me back my freedom. Now I am returning to your small village and your house, bringing the birds who are my family and friends, among others. We are coming to live here in your beautiful village—to share joy with you through our songs and chirps.

"It is God's will that we were created free, to enjoy the beauty of nature in our village and live together in peace."

Who Is the Worst Creature?

- LEBANON -

Salim was a young man who lived in a small village that sat at the heart of a kingdom in a beautiful land. He enjoyed being surrounded by the beauty of nature and listening to the songs of birds.

One day, Salim was walking along a favorite trail through the forest, when suddenly, he heard screaming coming from far ahead. Carefully, he started to walk toward the sound. The closer he got, the louder the screaming grew.

At last, Salim reached a bushy area. Walking toward the place where the screams were loudest, he discovered a very deep well. When he drew close to the well, he looked inside, and was surprised to find that a dog, a snake, a rat, and a man were trapped deep down inside the well, with no way to get out.

When those who were trapped in the well saw Salim's head appear in the light of the opening above them, they cried out even louder, "Please help us! Get us out of here! We're trapped!"

Salim, a courageous and helpful young man, went searching for a rope. He borrowed one from a nearby farmhouse and ran back to the well. Then he tied one end of the rope to a tree, and threw the other end down into the well.

"Grab onto the rope," he yelled, "and hang on!" Each time one of the captives got a good grip on the rope, Salim started pulling it up. The snake came out first. The dog came up next— and, finally, the rat.

Once the animals had been rescued, they turned to Salim and thanked him for saving their lives. Then they told him, "Don't bring up the man. He won't appreciate it."

Salim could see that they had been down there together for so long that the animals had come to know the man quite...well.

He wondered why the animals would tell him to leave the man stranded in that cold, dark place where he would certainly die. Salim was kindhearted and felt sorry for the man, so he threw down the end of the rope and pulled the man out.

After the man crawled out and over the lip of the well, he embraced Salim heartily, and said, "Thank you so much for saving my life. I promise to pay you back soon for your kindness."

The man was the only one to make this promise. Noticing this, Salim said to the animals, "I believe that you have misjudged the poor man who was in the well. I am glad that I saved him."

Time passed, and everyone carried on with their lives. One day, Dog went searching for Salim and found him hiking in the forest. Dog had brought a gift; it was a lamb from his flock to pay Salim back for saving his life! This reward made Salim feel so appreciated that he became good friends with Dog.

The next day, Dog told Rat where to find Salim. Rat, in turn, brought Salim a gift of wheat seeds to plant as a repayment for saving his life.

"Thank you," said Salim. "Your generous gift will help me to feed my family."

At first, Snake did not know what to get Salim, but finally, she thought of the perfect gift. In order to obtain this gift, Snake would have to sneak into the castle and reach its deepest chambers without making a sound or being seen. Carefully, after nightfall, Snake slithered through a hole in the wall of the castle and moved silently toward the princess's room. While the princess slept soundly in her bed, Snake took some of her jewelry to offer to her savior, Salim. The next day, Snake presented Salim with this precious gift.

Early the next morning, when the princess woke up and found her jewelry missing, her screams echoed around the rooms of the castle. All of the guards were alerted. They woke up the king and ran with him to the room of the princess to see what she was screaming about.

"Someone broke into my room and stole my jewelry while I slept!" the princess exclaimed.

Furious, the king turned to his guards and demanded, "Haste! Go find the thief who stole my daughter's jewelry. Bring him to me. Search every house and merchant's shop. Go…now!"

News of the theft quickly spread throughout the kingdom. Everyone learned that a bounty would be paid to the person who captured the thief.

Meanwhile, unaware of this commotion, Salim was walking around town wearing some of the jewelry that Snake had given him. He was pleased with all the rewards he had earned for saving the animals.

Unexpectedly, Salim bumped into the man he had pulled from the well. "I am glad to see you again, my friend," said the man. "I have not forgotten that you saved my life, and I promise to pay you back soon."

Before leaving each other's company, the man noticed that Salim was wearing an unusual garment adorned with some magnificent jewelry. Then the man thought to himself, "This is jewelry fit for a king."

After parting ways with Salim, the man went straight to the king and told him that he had found the man who had stolen the jewelry. The king sent his soldiers to capture Salim, so he could be brought to the gallows and hung.

Salim knew about the execution order. He learned that the man—whose life he had saved—had betrayed him to the king. When Salim was caught and brought to kneel before the king and his subjects, he remembered the words of his animal friends.

"Please, Majesty," Salim begged, "let me tell you the whole

story of what happened. I can explain everything."

The king looked down at Salim, and noticed that the young man had a kind and honest face. "Because you face such a grave penalty," answered the king, "I will allow you to speak."

Salim told his entire story in front of the king, and everyone who had gathered to witness the event.

After they had listened to Salim's story, the peasants turned toward the king and said, "We believe this man named Salim. We also know that his betrayer, the man he saved from the well, has done other bad deeds to our own kind in the past. Salim is innocent."

The king stood up and looked out over the crowd as he weighed the evidence in his mind. After a time, the king said, "Salim has shown only kindness to others, and has done nothing wrong. He is forgiven."

Then the king turned toward the man Salim had pulled from the well. "You, however, have been unfaithful to Salim, even after he saved your life. Your punishment will be one hundred days in the dungeon. You have set an example of how some people are the worst of the creatures God created."

Again addressing the crowd, the king said, "Observe how the animals have appreciated Salim's help more than this ungrateful man."

The king, with the blessing of his daughter, ruled that Salim deserved all of the rewards he had received from the animals.

Within the turn of a moon, the king also rewarded Salim with the greatest gift he had to offer any man. One evening, the king summoned Salim into his private chamber. "I would give to you my daughter's hand in marriage," said the king.

Salim was both shocked and excited to hear the king's offer. He had admired the princess from afar, for she was a beautiful and kindhearted young woman.

Salim waited for the right words to say. At last, he replied, "I am deeply moved, and would be most honored to accept this precious gift, Your Majesty. I will love your daughter well, and will treat her with kindness for all of our days together."

From that day forward, Salim and his princess bride lived happily ever after, with Rat, Dog, and Snake as their treasured, faithful friends.

Little green bee-eater *(Merops orientalis)*
(Photo by Dr. Anton Khalilieh)

Wisdom on the Wing

- PALESTINE -

There came a time when the rains failed and food was hard to find. A bird was out searching for something to feed her young chicks. She had not found anything to eat for many days, and her family was going hungry.

As the bird searched beneath a thicket for some grubs or seeds to eat, she became caught in a hunter's trap. The hunter was out chasing animals in the forest when he found the bird struggling to free itself. He bent down to look at the bird.

Feeling sad because there was no escape, the bird looked up at the hunter and said, "You are a generous person. As you can see, I am light and skinny, and there is not enough meat on my bones to satisfy your hunger."

"But I, too, am starving," answered the hunter.

"I can offer you something more valuable than food," said the bird.

"What could possibly be worth more than the food I need to stay alive?"

"I can give to you three nuggets of wisdom."

The hunter looked closely at the bird, and then he replied, "I can see that you are intelligent by the way you tried to escape my cage and flee. I am an experienced hunter who has learned much from life. You are arrogant to think you might have the knowledge and maturity to offer me advice."

"Listen first, then judge," responded the bird. "The clever man takes wisdom from God's smallest creatures."

"Very well," laughed the hunter, who was amused at the boldness of the little bird. "I am listening!"

"Before I offer this wisdom, you must agree to meet three conditions."

"Truly!?" exclaimed the hunter as he rocked back on his heels in surprise. He was now intrigued by the bird's rash confidence. "And what are these conditions of yours?"

"You must listen to the first nugget of wisdom while holding me in your hand. I will tell you the second bit of wisdom only after you allow me to perch on the branch of a tree. If you want the third, most valuable words of wisdom, you must allow me to fly into the sky."

Fascinated by whatever such a clever bird might have to tell him, the hunter thought, "I can be humble, open my heart, and listen to the bird's advice. Why not?!"

"Very well," said the hunter. He took the bird out of the cage and held her in his hand. "Let me hear the first bit of wisdom."

"So you agree!" said the bird as she stared deeply into the hunter's eyes. "Here is the first nugget of wisdom. Don't look back in regret, because regret brings to humankind nothing but misery and sadness, without changing the past."

As promised, the hunter let the bird go, and she flew up into a nearby tree. Happily perched on a branch, the bird offered her second morsel of wisdom, saying, "Don't believe everything you hear, or that which your mind doesn't grasp, especially nowadays, when the media cannot always be trusted to tell the truth."

Then the bird flew up in the sky. She soared in circles above the hunter, crying out, "I forgot to mention something important.

I swallowed a precious stone. If you had cut me open when you had the chance, you would have become a rich man!"

The hunter bit his finger and groaned with regret. Then he looked up and yelled, "Just tell me the third piece of your wisdom, and then leave me be."

The bird laughed and replied, "Judging by what you just said, and how you said it, you haven't listened to my first two nuggets of wisdom. How can you expect me to tell you the third? I told you not to regret anything, but you are feeling bad about letting me go. I told you not to believe everything you hear, and then you believed I had a precious stone inside of me, even though I am frail and thin."

Now the hunter saw the truth in what the bird was saying. He felt sad, nodded his head, and said, "You are right. I don't deserve the last nugget of wisdom. Now go. Just leave me alone."

Chukar partridge *(Alectoris chukar)*
(Photo by Dr. Anton Khalilieh)

The Garden of Wisdom

- ISRAEL-

A king once lived who said that people should not be given their position in life by birth or wealth. "It is my belief," he told his three sons, "that people should earn their standing in life according to who they have become and what they have accomplished by their own deeds. It does not matter to me into which family or kingdom a person is born, unless he has done something of value and nobility."

When the king's three sons were full-grown, he took them into his chamber and spoke. "As you know, you have, by birthright, been given much wealth and privilege. I love you all very much, my heart desires to keep you close, and there is much work to be done here in the kingdom. But it is time for you to go into the world and show me who you are and what you are capable of doing. Thus, I am sending you on a long journey. This is your chance to accomplish something of greatness, and prove that you are worthy of serving in a position of authority and responsibility. When the time comes, I will send a ship to bring you home."

"Father, we are ready and anxious for this journey to begin," said the princes.

In two days, the three princes found themselves sailing toward the land of the Moors. On the way, they spotted a lush, green island on which there was a beautiful walled garden. The great ship slipped into the harbor, and the princes rowed to shore. In front of the garden gate stood three guardians. As the princes approached, they were greeted by an ancient, stooped guard.

"You are welcome to enter this garden, where you will find many pleasures. You may stay for some time, but one day, you will have to leave."

Then a second guardian spoke to the young men. She was very sick, with bumps and sores on her skin. "This garden is here for those who enter to feast on the fruits and delights herein. You can take nothing with you when you leave."

When the princes looked at the third guardian, they saw that he was a clean, handsome man of about the same age as their father.

"Be careful, and keep safe your souls," said this guardian. "Eat only the sound, ripe fruit. Do not pick or eat any fruit that is not yet ready, or which has gone by and begun to spoil."

As they stepped through the garden gate, their eyes sparkled. Each tree was heavy with ripe, delicious fruit. Gems and pearls glistened from the ground, which was laced with streams and rivers like fingers of clean, pure water embracing the fertile green earth. When the princes tasted the water, they found that it was sweet nectar. Each prince began to wander around the garden on his own.

One of the brothers could not keep his eyes off of the colorful rubies, diamonds, sapphires, and countless other gems strewn upon the ground. He began to fill his pockets, and thought of how he could carry away enough wealth to last a lifetime. When his pockets were full, he removed his shirt, tied off the cuffs to make a sack, and filled it with riches. Next, he took off and filled his pants, then his briefs, socks, and cap. Soon, this prince was walking around naked, straining to carry his clothes laden with riches. The prince was so afraid that something might happen to his wealth that he hefted its great weight everywhere he went. He was so consumed with gathering and guarding his gems that he did not eat. In time, he grew pale, weak, and sickly.

The second prince wandered in search of the perfect piece of fruit, and the sweetest spring from which to quench his thirst. He became so completely lost in eating and drinking to satisfy his tongue that he did not notice how obese he was growing.

"Look at this!" said the third prince to his brothers. "See how many different kinds of trees and flowers grow in this garden. This plant smells like it could have healing properties. Here is a kind of mineral that I have never seen before! Who could have created such a perfect world of nature on this island?" But the two other princes were so absorbed in pursuing their pleasures that they did not hear their brother.

In time, the third prince saw how everything in the garden had its place, and that the workings of all the living things moved to the same rhythm in a dance of life. The streams and rivers were full during the months when the plants most needed the water to grow their flowers, fruit, and seeds. As he wandered and wondered at his surroundings, he ate and drank only what he needed to retain health and vigor, savoring every mouthful. "Some great, wise, unseen force must have created this glorious world," he thought. "It could not possibly have arisen by chance. If only there was someone here who could answer my questions."

One day, after several seasons had passed, a ship sailed into the harbor. The three brothers were called to the garden gate. A Moor, a messenger from their father, told the princes that the king had summoned them. "My sons, it is time for you to return home. You are to leave without haste, and return to the palace. Your ship awaits."

As the three princes left the garden, the guardians beat and mocked the one who was laboring under the weight of his jewels and gems. "Look how you have wasted away to nothing," they said. "And it was all for naught, because you cannot bring any of your treasure beyond these gates." At that, they wrestled all of the prince's wealth from him, and scattered it once again over the garden grounds.

As the three brothers rowed out to the ship that was waiting in the harbor, the one who had been eating and drinking for many months, and was enormously obese, collapsed and died of exertion.

When the two brothers reached the palace gates, the guards did not recognize the one who had wasted away as he gathered and hoarded his riches in the garden. In his grief over losing his fortune and being humiliated by the guardians of the garden, this prince had continued to neglect his body. When the guards refused to allow him to enter the palace, he began to cry and beg for them to allow him to pass. Even though the king sent a letter to the guards saying that this was his son, they drove him from the kingdom.

When the guards turned toward the third prince, they cried, "Welcome, Highness." This son was led with great dignity and celebration through the grounds of the palace and into the king's chamber.

The king rose and embraced the prince warmly, as tears welled up in his eyes and flowed down into his thick gray beard. "I am glad to have you home again, son."

"Father, I am glad to be home. You should have seen the island and the garden where we spent these many months. It is a beautiful place where the birds, animals, and plants live in complete harmony. Many things live there that we do not have in our kingdom. I wandered for months as I tried to understand how all of these things are able to live together so completely, and who could possibly have created such a wondrous place."

Again, the king held his son close and kissed him. "Sit, and I will answer all of your questions." For many hours, they met in quiet counsel as the king satisfied the prince's burning curiosity.

Finally, the king said to his son, "I am glad to see that you did not spend your time seeking earthly pleasures in the garden. Many people are only interested in gathering wealth during the course of their lives. In the end, these poor, empty lives have been wasted. Others are consumed with satisfying the pleasures of the body. Their lives are brief. You have chosen to find delight and meaning in understanding creation, and the mystery that lies beyond this world. Your reward will be great."

For Parents
& Teachers

SOURCES OF THE STORIES

Abu L'Hssein, the Generous (Egypt)
— As told by Michael J. Caduto

The Hoopoe's Crown (Israel)
— As told by Michael J. Caduto

What Really Happened? (Palestine)
— Shared by Nazih Moghrabi

The Story of the Baatharan Shrub
Artemisia judaica (Egypt)
— Shared by Sheikh Gamil Atteia Husein;
transcribed by Sara El Sayed

Qours Annee and the Rat (Lebanon)
— Shared by Mounir Abi Said

The Tree of a Life (Israel)
— As told by Michael J. Caduto

The Camel Who Saved Its Master (Egypt)
— Shared by Ahmed Eissa;
transcribed by Sara El Sayed

Raji over the Rainbow (Jordan)
— Shared by Nuha Hammoudeh;
translated by Hiba Rteil

The Well of Judgment (Palestine)
— Shared by Manal Ghneim

I Wonder Who It Will Be? (Palestine)
— Shared by Nazih Moghrabi

Thanking God for All Things (Egypt)
— Shared by Sheikh Gamil Atteia Husein;
transcribed by Sara El Sayed

Iman's Journey (Jordan)
— Shared by Rima K.

Saving the Cedars of Lebanon (Lebanon)
— Shared by Nizar Hani

Salma and Her Little Bird (Jordan)
— Shared by Manal Al-Foqaha;
translated by Hiba Rteil

Who Is the Worst Creature? (Lebanon)
— Shared by Mounir Abi Said

Wisdom on the Wing (Palestine)
— Shared by Manal Ghneim

The Garden of Wisdom (Israel)
— as told by Michael J. Caduto;
translated by Eli Rogosa

From herbalists among the Bedouin to educators, biologists, and keepers of traditional tales, the stories in *The Garden of Wisdom* have been gathered and shared by those who live close to nature in the Middle East. These children's stories are chosen to entertain and delight. Each tale also contains nuggets of truth that encourage children to learn about, and care for, our fragile Earth—the plants, animals, people, and natural resources that all forms of life rely upon for survival.

(Photo by Dr. Anton Khalilieh)

Woven into the threads of these traditional tales—and interlaced with a few modern twists—are the kinds of insights that come from time-tested knowledge and wisdom. At its heart, the story of "The Hoopoes Crown" is more than just a warning not to be vain and overly proud; it is a cautionary tale about the dangers of hunting a species to near-extinction. "Qours Annee and the Rat" and "The Story of the Baatharan Shrub" reveal the healing powers of plants. "I Wonder Who It Will Be" shows how throwing trash into the environment has a life-changing impact on a community of marine animals, and calls upon each of us to be hopeful and take action to repair the damage that people do to the environment. The story of "Abu L'Hssein, the Generous" demonstrates how each animal, in its own way, is uniquely adapted to survive in its particular environment. In "The Tree of a Life," we witness how each generation can work to make the world a better place for children to come. "The Garden of Wisdom" reminds us to observe and appreciate the wonders and beauties in nature.

A number of stories feature girls and women who are strong and wise. The main character in "Iman's Journey" is a courageous young girl who defeats a group of boys who are bullying other children and nature. Iman also teaches the boys not to hurt anyone—especially birds, animals, and other children. Wily and wise tricksters appear in many guises, such as the bird who fools a man in "Wisdom on the Wing." Woven throughout the book are wonderful (and sometimes magical) characters, whose exploits teach us about the importance of caring for Earth, resisting those who harm the natural world, safeguarding one another's freedom, and the power of friendship, gratitude, faith, and love.

Over time, we plan to translate and publish *The Garden of Wisdom* in Arabic and Hebrew. We also intend to create teacher's guides in various languages. These guides will use the subjects raised in the stories as an invitation for further exploration through study questions, background information, and hands-on activities for children.

In order to make the world a better place for the youth of today and tomorrow, it is essential that children appreciate the natural world and understand the many ways in which they are connected to nature. We can give children the knowledge and skills they need to protect their environment. These stories show how stewardship can be fun, entertaining, and empowering.

Students participate in an avian research program through the Palestine Wildlife Society. (Photo courtesy Sami Backleh)

LESSONS TAUGHT BY THE STORIES

Abu L'Hssein, the Generous (Egypt) — Each animal has its own distinct physical adaptations and behaviors that enable it to survive. If you play tricks on others, they could play tricks on you. Maintaining a sense of humor and equality is essential for an enduring friendship. Our differences make us unique.

The Hoopoe's Crown (Israel) — Doing a good deed for another can lead to receiving a gift in return. Indulging in vanity and pride can lead to bad things happening. People often envy those who have more possessions than they do. Animals that possess something that people find to be beautiful or useful are often at risk. Trading parts of animals for profit often leads to overhunting and poaching, causing species endangerment and extinction. Endangered animals can grow in number once they are no longer being hunted. Storytelling is one way of explaining natural phenomena.

What Really Happened? (Palestine) — Traditionally, wells are both sources of water and gathering places at the heart of a community. Observing, listening carefully, and communicating clearly are essential to telling the truth. A story often grows in the telling. An outside observer can often see things more clearly. A leader keeps a cool head in the face of a threat, and maintains a sense of humor. At the end of the day, honesty will be rewarded.

The Story of the Baatharan Shrub (Egypt) — People's needs can be met by gathering resources from their environment and creating something useful (for example, making charcoal from dry twigs). Certain species of wild plants, when prepared in a particular way and used wisely, can heal sickness. Using plants for healing is a tradition among the Bedouin of the Sinai. *It is extremely important to know the exact identity of a species of wild plant, and to be certain that plant is safe, before using it for food or medicine.*

Qours Annee and the Rat (Lebanon) — Some plants have medicinal powers. Observing plants and animals, and drawing careful conclusions, can lead to new discoveries about the natural world. Employing trial and error is one way of conducting a scientific experiment. Conducting an experiment on another living being can cause injury or death, and lead to regret.

The Tree of a Life (Israel) — Water is critical for growing crops and surviving in the desert. In times of extreme drought, there is a tradition of looking for help from people believed to have the power to speak to God and bring the rain. Desert rains bring on the sudden growth and flowering of plants. Planting trees, along with other good acts to grow beneficial things, will provide for future generations. Don't sleep your life away!

The Camel Who Saved Its Master (Egypt) — Friendship can form between people and the animals they care for. It is important to observe the weather and predict its impact upon your environment. It is possible to carry on in life, stay hopeful, and keep faith after losing someone you have cared for deeply. Discipline, tempered by compassion, is important when training and caring for animals. Wild plants can be used for medicine and healing. In times of crisis, acting swiftly and wisely is critical. *It is extremely important to know the exact identity of a species of wild plant, and to be certain that plant is safe, before using it for food or medicine.*

Raji over the Rainbow (Jordan) — True friendship and peaceful coexistence require thinking about the needs and wants of others, sharing what we have to give, and forgiving others their faults and slights to one's pride. When a person is lonely, they still need to grow friendships based upon mutual trust and respect. Selfishness can be harmful to relationships with others. Sometimes, one needs to reach out to others with an open heart in order to mend a wounded friendship. Being

kind to a younger sibling requires patience and love. Children can learn much about life by listening to their parents. Meaningful symbols, like the rainbow, can become teachers that guide us on our path through life.

The Well of Judgment (Palestine) — Littering damages the environment and has to be cleaned up by others. Cooperating with others can help make the land productive and beautiful. It takes hard work and patience to grow food. In stories, owls often appear as wise. The truth will eventually be discovered; friends will forgive other friends.

I Wonder Who It Will Be? (Palestine) — A single piece of trash can alter an environment and harm the lives of the animals and plants that live there. Fish and other animals have lives of their own that are impacted by human activity. Aquatic environments are fragile and easily damaged. A single event can be the start of something much larger to come. Leadership often comes to one who has vision—the ability to see the big picture and inspire others to play a role in stopping whatever is harming the environment.

Thanking God for All Things (Egypt) — Having faith means showing gratitude for the gifts of creation. Respecting and caring for elders is an honored tradition. Being patient and taking care of those you love is hard work.

Being selfish, and not thanking God, can bring bad fortune. Issuing an ultimatum can backfire. One sometimes needs to question another closely in order to discover the truth. Keeping faith and giving thanks to God leads to good things in life. One cannot turn back the hands of time.

Iman's Journey (Jordan) — It is important to have courage and believe in one's own ability to stand up to injustice, especially when confronting long odds of success. Raising girls and boys as equals is important for nurturing the healing power and sense of justice that everyone brings into the world. There is strength in standing up to those who bully other people and the natural world. There is a strong connection between how we treat nature and how we treat our fellow human beings. Setting a positive example leads others to follow. Forgiving and offering a second chance to those who have done wrong opens an opportunity for reform and reconciliation. Playing sports strengthens a child's body, mind, and spirit. Faith gives us power. Girls with superpowers rock!

Saving the Cedars of Lebanon (Lebanon) — For those who listen to nature, there is wisdom to be found in an ancient tree. The actions of people can threaten the existence of species and habitats. Human conflict causes great harm to the natural world. It takes leadership, caring, and hard work to restore a forest. Nature can be saved when people cooperate and work together in peace. The future is in our hands.

Salma and Her Little Bird (Jordan) — Extending oneself to help another in need is often rewarded in unexpected ways. True friendship, empathy, and stewardship are rooted in understanding the needs and wants of another. It is important to listen to the wisdom of our elders. Making the right decision for someone we love sometimes means suffering a loss to ourselves. True friendship is found with those who choose to be our friends. Relationships are a circle of giving and receiving. Happiness is rooted in freedom. Our sacrifices are rewarded in ways that we could not possibly have imagined.

Who Is the Worst Creature? (Lebanon) — It is a virtue to help others in need. Listen to the opinions of others, but trust in your own judgment. Not everything is as it appears. Friendship can be complicated. We reap what we sow. Justice requires an open mind and careful consideration of the facts. True friendship is based on appreciation and reciprocity.

Wisdom on the Wing (Palestine) — A sharp wit can carry someone far in the world. Keep an open mind when listening to others, and do not judge by appearance. Listen and think carefully before taking action. Don't believe everything you hear. Look forward (not backward) with the goal of learning from past mistakes, and use these lessons to do better next time. Know when to accept what has happened, and when to move on. Wisdom can be found in unexpected places.

The Garden of Wisdom (Israel) — It brings joy to appreciate and observe the wonders and beauties of nature, and to give thanks for the gifts we receive from creation. The decisions we make in our lifetimes determine who we will become. Taking care of one's own body and soul honors creation. Everything in the natural world is connected, and moves together in a dance of life. Seeking wealth and pleasure for their own sake can lead to neglecting one's own well-being. Wisdom is both a gift and an act of will—it is a virtue that is valued and nurtured over time, and is its own reward.

THE JOURNEY BEHIND THE STORIES
- EXPLORING NATURE IN THE MIDDLE EAST -
by Michael J. Caduto

In April of 2007, the Israel Nature and Parks Authority (INPA) and the Palestine Wildlife Society invited me to explore natural areas in the heart of the Middle East, and to experience firsthand the region's environmental issues. Soon after arriving, I received a whirlwind tour of the hillsides and villages bordering Tel Aviv, followed by a wonderful meal and an evening of storytelling. The next morning, I was whisked off to the town of Beit Sahour in the West Bank to meet with staff of the Palestine Wildlife Society (PWLS). There, in an office set in the middle of a bustling neighborhood, I encountered a wealth of ongoing environmental education programs and publications, then toured the West Bank to see the impact of human encroachment on dwindling pockets of wildlife habitat. On one particularly poignant stop along the way, Imad Atrash, Executive Director of the PWLS, gestured out toward a patch of scrub forest in a small valley, and told the story of how the last remaining deer living in that region had been hunted just years before.

Over the course of the following week, INPA staff led me on a guided tour of Israeli sites and borderlands that embody critical natural areas and key environmental issues. I encountered a magnificent landscape, rich in

biological diversity because it lies at the convergence of Europe, Asia, and Africa. From snowcapped mountains and vast deserts to expansive lakes and marine ecosystems, few places on Earth possess this startling array of habitats and species in such a small geographic area as the Middle East.

Wild goat *(Capra aegagrus)*
(Photo by Elad Topel)

Nature's grandeur is juxtaposed with vivid examples of the impact that people have had over time. En route to Gamla Nature Reserve in the Golan Heights, north of the Sea of Galilee, we drove through grassy swells denuded of forest centuries ago. Pastoral hills

141

were fenced and marked with signs warning of minefields never cleared—a vestige of past wars.

Along the dizzying cliffs in Gamla, griffon vultures rose on thermals, so close that we could almost touch these ancient birds, whose wingspan exceeds eight feet. This, the largest breeding colony of vultures in Israel, is in rapid decline. Many eggs are infertile, and numerous hatchlings die due to a calcium-poor diet and lack of food (dead animal carcasses) in the wild. Adult vultures can't obtain enough calcium from small pieces of dead animal bones, so they feed instead upon the metal fragments of old ammunition and shrapnel that litter the countryside. Vultures die by electrocution when they perch on power lines, as a result of intentional shootings, and by inadvertent killings when they feed on the remains of cattle poisoned by farmers locked in territorial dispute. Later, at the Hai Bar ("live wild") Carmel Nature Reserve, a lanky, bearded naturalist named Ygal Miller proudly told of how he established the first successful captive breeding and release program for griffon vultures.

We drove south, past Bedouin riding donkeys while grazing sheep and camels at the edge of the Judean Desert. Well below sea level, we stood in an abandoned dining room framed by the mortar-riddled walls of the old Jordan Hotel, and looked across a vast plain that dipped toward the distant shoreline of the Dead Sea. Before the hotel was aban-

Griffon vulture (*Gyps fulvus*)
(Photo by Dr. Anton Khalilieh)

doned during the 1967 war, waves still lapped at the feet of guests who stood on this veranda. Dead Sea water is now being drastically drawn down and desalinated to quench the thirst of this densely-populated region.

As peace efforts continue, the viability of ecosystems and resources also stands at a crossroads that will determine environmental health and the survival of many species. The demise of the Dead Sea would devastate Jordanians, Israelis, and Palestinians alike. Invasive plants out-compete native species that provide nesting sites for birds, plus food and shelter for animals. Many plants and animals are collected, hunted, and poached toward endangerment and extinction. On most days, in the hills of the Carmel Coast, polluted air hangs so thick it is impossible to see the Med-

142

iterranean Sea just two to three miles away. Water pollution, depletion of precious water supplies, and degradation of habitat for migratory birds are serious problems.

In the Middle East, environmental issues pose the greatest long-term threat to the health and well being of humans and the natural world. Private organizations and governmental agencies are conducting critical environmental research and conservation programs. They also teach of the necessity of adapting policies and practices that will preserve the habitats and natural resources essential to the survival of all forms of life. The environment is the one tie that irrevocably binds the peoples of the Middle East, regardless of differences in politics, faith, or culture.

Overgrazing by goats and other domesticated animals is a major threat to natural habitats throughout the Middle East. (Photo by Dr. Anton Khalilieh)

In light of the need to solve these environmental problems, the Quebec-Labrador Foundation/Atlantic Center for the Environment (QLF) launched the Stories for Environmental Stewardship Program (SES Program), a collaborative effort to address environmental issues through storytelling, environmental education, and stewardship. This groundbreaking program—the first of its kind in the region—brings together the experience and expertise of QLF alumni, both in the United States and throughout the Middle East.

The leaves of this book bear the fruit that has grown from twenty years of collaborative professional relationships cultivated by QLF, a non-governmental organization based in Ipswich, Massachusetts. Growing from these roots, the SES Program has brought together conservationists, educators, storytellers, and biologists who have gathered stories from among the peoples living in Egypt, Israel, Jordan, Lebanon, and Palestine.

The Stories for Environmental Stewardship Program is a non-political means of working with peoples of the region to enhance the teaching of traditional knowledge by adding a stewardship component: stories that inspire and encourage wisdom as a foundation for positive behavior toward the environment. To these ends, the SES Program strives to combine indigenous stories and environmental activities with an understanding of contemporary environmental issues.

Stories explore people's relationship with the natural world; they are a powerful educational tool for integrating the social and cultural values of Middle Eastern society and culture with regard to the importance of the natural environment.

> *"Stories are the secret reservoir of values: change the stories individuals and nations live by and tell themselves, and you change the individuals and nations."*
> — Ben Okri, Nigerian author & winner of the Booker Prize

The Garden of Wisdom: Earth Tales from the Middle East uses the ancient practice of transmitting knowledge to each new generation by telling folkloric stories that are often shared during social gatherings. These stories have been remembered by each generation, and handed down to children through oral tradition. Stories that are mastered and retold to children from memory are time-honored threads from which the fabric of culture is woven.

Disseminating folklore stories with a clear conservation message and combining them with complementary environmental activities can raise the awareness levels of participants, and help them to become conservationists without borders. Time and again, these stories have proven that the wisdom of the ages transcends the boundaries by which we define the geography of our physical world and the realm of our inner being.

Environmental stories and activities are used in many countries to encourage the growth of positive environmental values and behavior among young children. Stories are also used to inform and influence environmental knowledge, skills, and stewardship among older children. For adults, whose lives are immersed in their own particular social and cultural milieu, environmental stories can form a bridge between time-honored customs and the importance of preserving natural surroundings and vital resources.

> *"The only myth that is going to be worth thinking about in the immediate future is the one that is talking about the planet."*
> — Joseph Campbell, *The Power of Myth*

White stork (*Ciconia ciconia*)
(Photo by Dr. Anton Khalilieh)

In this anthology, *The Garden of Wisdom: Earth Tales from the Middle East*, many traditional and contemporary stories have been gathered from oral tradition. The stories were then translated (when necessary), edited, and retold so as to reflect the voice of the original storyteller.

Accompanying teacher's guides will be created during the second phase of the SES Program. The stories will be complemented by background information about the natural world and the environmental issues they introduce. Environmental activities addressing these issues will be developed and field-tested. The stories, information, and activities will be arranged according to the natural history and environmental issues explored within each section, reflecting the interrelated lands and peoples of the Middle East, regardless of cultural or political boundaries. When completed, the teacher's guides will be published and made available to schools, private organizations, public agencies, educators, and families within the host countries.

It is our aspiration that the Stories for Environmental Stewardship Program will continue to foster peacebuilding relationships among environmental education professionals and organizations throughout the Middle East, and that it will grow to engage other peoples within this broad, interconnected bioregion.

— Michael J. Caduto, Director
Stories for Environmental
Stewardship Program

The Stories for Environmental Stewardship Program began with a simple telephone call from Jessica Brown, who was then serving as the senior vice president for international programs at the Quebec-Labrador Foundation/Atlantic Center for the Environment (QLF). Jessica asked if I would like to facilitate a seminar on environmental education at QLF's First Alumni Congress in April of 2006. My thanks to Jessica for presenting me with the opportunity to meet and work with many colleagues from the Middle East who have since made the SES Program possible.

A special thanks to Tammy Keren-Rotem, National Director of Environmental Education Programs, Israel Nature and Parks Authority (INPA). It was during the aforementioned seminar that Tammy originally suggested that QLF alumni could work together as partners to gather environmental stories from throughout the Middle East. Tammy also served as co-director of the SES Program for several years.

The unflagging support of two people, in particular, has been critical to the birth, growth, and final success of the SES Program: Larry Morris, President Emeritus, Quebec-Labrador Foundation; and Beth Alling, President and CEO of QLF. Larry and Beth have always been there, offering support behind the scenes for a period of more than ten years, which encompassed many meetings, overseas trips, and hundreds of emails and phone calls. If ever a project existed for which the phrase "I couldn't have done it without you" was true, this has been that project.

Financial backing for the SES Program has come from the Quebec-Labrador Foundation's Middle East Program (with funding from the Feather Foundation), and also from a Brimstone Grant, as administered by the National Storytelling Network. I am grateful to both organizations for their support. Members of the National Storytelling Network's Brimstone Committee, especially storyteller Sarah Mutziger, demonstrated unwavering faith in the promise of the SES Program. Several colleagues offered their support during the fundraising process, including Diane Edgecomb, storyteller and author; Catherine O'Brian, coordinator of arts education grants and programs for the New Hampshire State Council on the Arts; and QLF alumnae Rosemary Furfey and Diane Hewlett-Lowrie. Thank you, also, to these major individual supporters: Kathleen Dolan, Jameson French, Donna Hollinger, Charlotte Metcalf, Magda Nassef, and Mary Kay Swider.

Trips to the Middle East were facilitated by Tammy Keren-Rotem and Sami Backleh, biodiversity consultant and regional coordinator for QLF's Middle East Conservation

Exchange Program. I am most grateful to the following people for their generous hospitality during my 2007 tour of Israel and the West Bank to study natural areas and environmental issues in the region: Imad F. Atrash, Executive Director, Palestine Wildlife Society; Ron Elan, Esquire; Yael Gavrieli, Ph.D. and Director, Nature Campus, Tel Aviv University, Israel; Ran Levy-Yamamori, children's author; and Salman Abu Rukun, Director of the Educational and Guidance Division of the INPA. Logistical help was also provided by Agi Simon of QLF Special Projects, Atlantic Region and International, and by Nancy J. Malaquias, Program Assistant for QLF.

I want to thank my wife, Marie Levesque Caduto, for supporting and believing in this project, even when I was heading off for another trip or otherwise absent at home while in pursuit of an elusive contact or story.

Sami Backleh and Elizabeth Alling were instrumental during my search for stories and storytellers in the Middle East, from whom rich folklore has been featured in this collection, including tales from the peoples of Egypt, Israel, Jordan, Lebanon, and Palestine. Hiba Rteil, M.S. in Environmental Management, employed her keen mind for languages to translate several Jordanian and Palestinian stories from Arabic into English. Eli Rogosa, friend and founder of the Heritage Grain Conservancy, helped to locate and translate a Hebrew version of "The Garden of Wisdom" story while she was working in Israel.

Many people generously offered their help and time to make contacts and facilitate the gathering of stories and imagery from the field, including Manal Al-Foqaha, Trainer and Community Mobilizer at the Jordan River Foundation (Jordan River Children Program); Sara El Sayed, Senior School Coordinator, Wadi Environmental Science Centre, Giza, Egypt; QLF's Sami Backleh; Sharón Benheim, Ben Gurion University of the Negev Conflict Management and Resolution Program; and Anne-Seymour St. John, who carried out the pilot Middle East Program in 1992, and serves as senior advisor.

In addition, my gratitude goes out to all whose ideas helped to guide the SES Program during its formative stages, including Amr Ali, Managing Director, Hurghada Environmental Protection and Conservation Association; Ibrahim Odeh, Director, Department of Environmental Education, Palestine Wildlife Society; and Ra'ed Abu Hayyaneh, Regional Director of Programs & Projects, ArabEnv, Amman, Jordan.

My deepest appreciation and gratitude to Odelia Liphshiz for creating the astonishingly beautiful and vivid illustrations that illuminate each story in this book, bringing the characters and the beauty of nature to life on the page. And thank you to the photographers who generously contributed their creative talents through images that immerse readers in the natural world of the Middle East: Dr. Anton Khalilieh, Dr. Elaine Solowey, and Elad Topel. The striking end papers, reproduced from original designs hand-painted in the 1860s, were generously provided by Mary Louise Pierson, artist and photographer: www.mlpierson.com. Douglas Lufkin of Lufkin Graphic Designs deftly wove all of these images with the text to create this elegant, expressive book.

Of course, there would be no stories without those who dedicate their lives to keeping oral tradition alive through their work as educators, artists, and supporters of community enrichment. My heartfelt thanks to all who contributed stories for the SES stories collection: Mounir R. Abi-Said, Ph.D., mammalogist, Director of Biodiversity Management, Biology Dept./FAS, American University of Beirut, and Director of Animal Encounter; Aley-Ras El-Jabal (Lebanon); Ahmen Eissa (Egypt); Manal Al-Foqaha (Jordan); Manal Ghneim, storyteller and theater educator, Tamer Institute for Community Education (Jerusalem); Nuha Hammoudeh (Jordan); Nizar Hani, scientific coordinator, and Kamal Abou Assi, Communication and Ecotourism Coordinator, Shouf Biosphere Reserve/ Al Shouf Cedar Nature Reserve (Lebanon); Sheikh Gamil Atteia Husein, Egypt; Rima K. (Jordan); and Nazih Moghrabi, artist and music teacher, St. George School (Jerusalem).

They are all passionate lovers of nature who have sown and nurtured the seeds that yielded a rich harvest of stories in *The Garden of Wisdom.*

ABOUT THE EDITOR AND ILLUSTRATOR

(Photo courtesy Greg Nesbit Photography. © 2011)

Michael J. Caduto, author, environmental educator, storyteller, and ecologist, is well known as the creator and co-author (with Joseph Bruchac) of the best-selling *Keepers of the Earth*® series. His articles have been published by Reuters International and in major newspapers and magazines, including *Haaretz*. Michael's latest books are *Through a Naturalist's Eyes, Riparia's River,* and *Catch the Wind, Harness the Sun: 22 Supercharged Science Projects for Kids*. He has received the Brimstone Award, the Teacher's Choice Award, the Aesop Prize, the Storytelling World Award, and the NAPPA Gold Award. Michael's model for integrating storytelling and environmental education was published by UNESCO-UNEP as *A Guide on Environmental Values*

Education and has been translated into English, French, and Spanish. His programs and publications are described on his website at www.p-e-a-c-e.net.

(Photo courtesy Odelia Liphshiz)

Odelia Liphshiz is an accomplished illustrator and artist based in Israel. She creates worlds of fantasy and wonder for children, and for everyone who is a child at heart. Odelia has illustrated children's books for A.A Milne, Nurit Zarchi, and more. Says Odelia, "I am a peace-seeker, dreamer, and a great believer." More of her work can be found at www.Odelialeaf.com.

CPSIA information can be obtained
at www.ICGtesting.com
Printed in the USA
BVOW05*0030221217

503433BV00006B/8/P